Around Liverpool and Merseyside

in the 1960s

Clive Hardy

iNostalgia

Around Liverpool and Merseyside in the 1960s

(Above). Ford production line at Halewood, 23 January 1967.

(Opposite page). Queen Elizabeth II and Prince Philip arrive at Liverpool Lime Street Station for an evening engagement at the start of their visit to Lancashire. May 1961.

Clive Hardy

© 2017 Text Clive Hardy

ISBN 978-1-84547-243-6

© Photographs: Liverpool Echo, Mirrorpix, Clive Hardy.

Designed by Clive Hardy.

Clive Hardy has asserted his rights under Copyright, Designs and Patents Act, 1988, to be identified as the author of this work.

iNostalgia Ltd, Progress Centre, Charlton Place, Ardwick, Manchester M12 6HS. UK.

Admiral of the Fleet Earl Mountbatten takes the salute at the 25th anniversary of the Battle of the Atlantic ceremony from the steps of the Anglican Cathedral. May 1968.

(Opposite). A dumped car gets a going over. Kirkby, 18 March 1965.

Introduction

Welcome to *Around Merseyside in the 1960s*, a snapshot in words and pictures of a decade when Liverpool registered ships sailed the oceans, Merseybeat took the world by storm and Liverpool, along with Salford, Manchester and Glasgow, was battling to clear away the worst slums in western Europe.

The area covered within these pages comprises the five metropolitan boroughs of Liverpool, St Helens, Sefton, Knowsley and the Wirral. We have not grouped the pictures geographically, instead they are divided into topic-related sections. So here we go with a brief introduction to some of the things you will come across in the following 92 pages.

The first section, *A Look at Life*, takes us through slum clearance and redevelopment, the changing face of Liverpool city centre, the Henderson's Department Store fire in June 1960, the completion of the Roman Catholic Metropolitan Cathedral of Christ The King and the topping out of St John's Beacon.

Next, we look at *The World of Work*. Cammell Laird Shipyard and the launchings of the destroyer *HMS Devonshire*, the tanker *British Ensign* and the nuclear-powered ballistic missile submarine *HMS Renown*. We also have the National Union of Seamen's strike –

which by the time it ended saw more than 800 ocean-going vessels laid up in British ports. From there, we have the docks, Ford Halewood, the NHS and the post.

On the Move includes the *Empress of Canada* and Blue Funnel's *Centaur* leaving the Mersey on their maiden voyages, the Mersey ferries, United Airlines' hovercraft service between the Wirral and Rhyl and the Everton team departing Lime Street on their way to the 1966 FA Cup Final. We also have the last steam-hauled passenger train operated by British Rail in August 1968, Sir John Moores and his Roller and so on.

Rock, Pop and Merseybeat includes Billy Fury's Rock 'n Trad Spectacular, the Vernons Girls, the Three Bells, the Escorts at the Cavern, Rory Storm and the Hurricanes, Cilla, Gerry and the Pacemakers', Swinging Blue Jeans, the Searchers, the Kinsleys, the Scaffold and, of course, The Beatles. From outside Merseyside we have the Dave Clark Five and the Rolling Stones at New Brighton.

That's Entertainment includes pensioners on a day out in New Brighton, the Liverpool Playhouse, Ken Dodd, and Jimmy Tarbuck. From the movies, we go on set with Cilla and the Fourmost in Gerry and the Pacemaker's *Ferry 'Cross the Mersey*.

We're also with Rita Tushingham on the set of *A Taste of Honey*. There are several images relating to the northern premier of *A Hard Day's Night*.

From entertainment we move to sport with individual sections on Everton, Liverpool and Tranmere Rovers. With so much to go at, the selection for inclusion in this publication had to be boiled down. For example, it would be possible to fill a book of this size solely with images and information on Liverpool's European cup competitions. So, for Everton, we have photographs from several League games, their 1966 and 1968 FA Cup campaigns as well as several players. Similarly, the photographs of Liverpool cover their game against Arsenal in what was the very first BBC TV Match of the Day, their 1965 FA Cup Final clash against Leeds United and a couple of League games from 1969. For Tranmere Rovers we have photographs from their 1967-68 FA Cup Fourth Round victory over Coventry City and subsequent Fifth Round match against Everton.

In *Grandstand?* we have images from several Grand Nationals, the 1961 British Grand Prix, Widnes Rugby League Football Club's Challenge Cup Final against Hull Kingston Rovers, boxing and the 1965 British Open Golf Championship and 16th Ryder Cup from Royal Birkdale.

There are some colour images. The 1960s was a time when newspapers were only just beginning to take some colour photographs. The majority of papers simply lacked the equipment to print in colour but occasionally colour photographs were taken, and readers could go along and buy a print.

Just a word of two about prices and costings you might come across in the book. They are given in pounds, shillings and pence with the metric equivalent in brackets where necessary. However, you will need to use the inflation calculator to bring them up to 2017 levels. For example, an item costing £1.10s.0d (£1.50p) in 1962 needs to be multiplied by 20.11 to bring it to its 2017 cost of £30.16 – you might need to round up or down. During the 1960s, prices could be written several ways but they all meant the same, so £1.10s.0d (£1.50p) could be written as £1/10/0 or £1/10/- or 30/¬ (thirty shillings), similarly 6s.9d (34p) could be written as 6/9d, or 6/9.

Conversions are: 6d = 2.5p; 1 shilling = 5p; half-a-crown or 2s.6d or 2/6d = 12.5p; 5s.0d or 5/- = 25p; 10s.0d or 10/- = 50p; £1.0s.0d or £1/-/- = 100p. By the late 60s, specialist outlets as well as family-run corner shops could trade on Sundays. Some prices are given in guineas, a guinea being 21/- (twenty-one shillings) or £1.1s.0d (£1.5p) and a half guinea was 10s.6d or 10/6 (52.5p). So, three guineas £3.3s.0d (£3.15p) would be written either as 3gns or 3Gns.

Also, a price say of seven and a half guineas translates to £7.17s.6d (£17.88p). To find its 2017 equivalent multiply £17.88 by 15.66. The inflation calculator for the decade is: 1960 21.01; 1961 20.80; 1962 20.11; 1963 19.28; 1964 18.91; 1965 18.30; 1966 17.46; 1967 16.81; 1968 16.40 and 1969 15.66. Have fun.

As we always state, these books are not academic works, nor can we cover everything. That would still be an impossibility even if we had a thousand pages to fill. So, put the cat out and the kettle on. Sit back, turn the pages and enjoy our look at what was and is *Around Merseyside in the 1960*s.

Acknowledgements

Charlie Owens, Cyril Maitland, MacDonald Alis, Howard Booth, Geoff Thomas, Neil Barkla, David Kemp, Gordon Whiting, Dave Horridge, Ken Jones, Jack Spencer, D A Wright, Bob Bird, Ian Kelso, Michael Charters, Frank McGee, Mike Ellis, Horace Yates, Arthur Sidney.

Special thanks to John Mead, Simon Flavin and Vito Inglese at Mirrorpix.

HMS Revenge gets a wash and brush-up in preparation for her commissioning at Cammell Laird on 4 December 1969.

A Look at Life

Slums off Great Homer Street, Everton. All the images are thought to date from early 1960, though they were published in the *Liverpool Echo* at different dates. More than 100,000 people were in need of rehousing and proposed redevelopment schemes over the coming decade or so would see 48,000 moved to Skelmersdale, 18,000 to Widnes, 19,350 to Halewood and 30,000 to Kirkby. In many areas, once close-knit communities were ripped apart as families, friends and neighbours were scattered and workers who had once lived close to their places of employment wee now faced with commuting.

A couple of years previously, the *Echo* had reported that families being moved out of the worst slums might be temporarily housed on three old P&O liners, the *Strathmore, Stratheden* and *Orion*, until their new homes were ready.

Bessie Braddock MP on a visit to one of Liverpool's slum clearance/redevelopments areas in June 1962. Born in Zante Street, Liverpool, in 1899, Braddock, who had honed her political skills as a councillor, was elected MP for Liverpool Exchange in the Labour landslide of 1945.

A great campaigner on housing, health and social welfare, she was a formidable lady and combative politician. In 1952 she became the first female MP to be suspended from the House after protesting, somewhat forthrightly, that the Speaker had failed to call her during a debate on the textile industry. At the time, the plight of the textile trade was of great concern to her constituents. From 1953 to 1957, she served on the Royal Commission for Mental Health, whose findings led to the Mental Health Act 1959.

She served as MP for Liverpool Exchange from 1945 until 1970. She was Liverpool's first woman freeman.

Redevelopment comes to the Sampson Street and Kapler Street area of Everton. Rehousing schemes effectively hollowed out the population of central Liverpool by tens of thousands of people.

The New Strand development at Bootle comprised a shopping centre with apartments above the shops and a 22-storey tower block. The image dates from June 1967. High-rise was politically expedient – and cheap. But even by the mid-1960s it was not turning out to be the revolution in social housing that the planners and architects had thought it would be. Many were poorly designed, the quality of the construction questionable and structural faults abounded; the proof of which was borne out during 1969, when a gas explosion caused an entire corner of the twenty-three storey Ronan Point tower block to collapse. In some boroughs no one seemed to be responsible for public areas. With council cleansing departments refusing to take responsibility and the very nature of the blocks putting tenants off from doing the job themselves, landings became litter traps. Stairwells and lifts stank of urine and, in some towers, there were serious problems with vermin infestation.

(Opposite) Living the dream in November 1969? All things electric appear to be the order of the day. The 1969 prices for some of these items were: portable telly £83.10s.0d (£83.50p), electric oven £180.0s.0d, portable record player £32.0s.0d, two-bar electric fire £15.15s.0d (£15.75p) and tumble dryer at £115.0s.0d. In some outlets, the price of the two-bar electric fire would have been displayed as 15Gns (fifteen guineas).

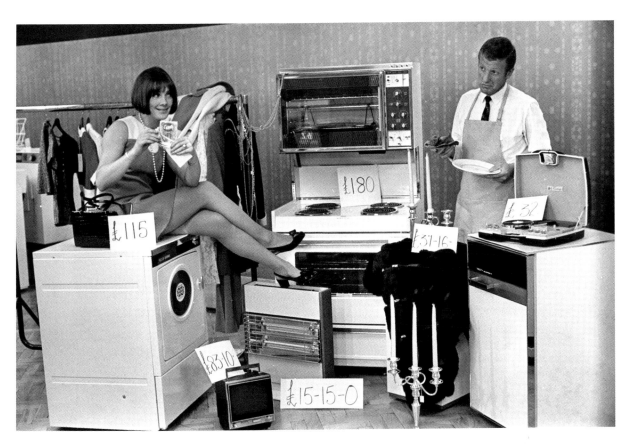

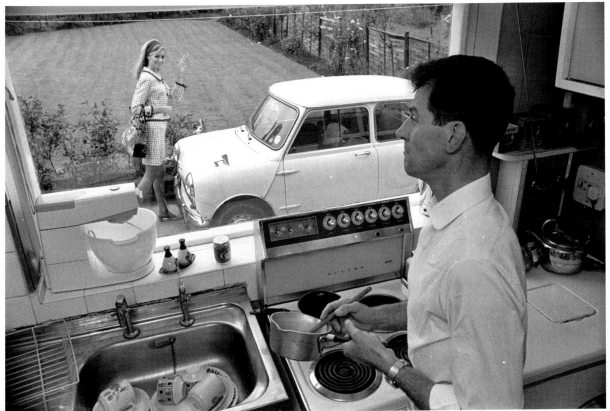

(Top Right) In the 1960s, numerous nationwide high street chains had branches along Lord Street, Liverpool, including Hardy & Co, Willerbys, Stead & Simpson and Telefusion. If you were setting up house during the 1960s and had money to spend on stuff, a 3yds x 2yds rug would set you back £3.19s.6d, carpeting cost anywhere between 9s.6d (47.5p) and £1.10s.0d (£1.50p) per square yard and a bedroom suite (double door ladies, double door gent's wardrobes plus dressing table with full landscape mirror) £34.2s.6d (£34.12.5p).

(Middle) Passers-by take a sneak look at what's on offer at the new Woollies store on London Road, Liverpool, on 14 November 1962. Inside, the store was on the final countdown to opening. Staff were busily filling shelves whilst manager Barry Jones and staff superintendent Mrs Elsie Travis were giving the rosters a final look-over and praying everything was covered.

(Bottom) Pram jam outside Woollies in Kirkby on 5 August 1964, following a request from the store for prams and pushchairs (this is in pre-buggy days) not to be left in the doorways.

(Opposite page bottom). 'Christmas is coming and the geese are getting fat.' Chickens, capons and turkeys are on offer at prices ranging from 12/6 to 16/-. That's 62.5p to 80p in funny money, but to get the 2017 price you will need to multiply by 16.88.

Kirkby's town market on 26 April 1961. The Sixties was the decade when those who had a little spare cash started going out for a meal – and not just fish and chips. Berni Inns, the Forte chain and Pizza Express were launched. An exotic sounding Pizza Margherita would have cost you 5s.6d (27.5p) and a bottle of red house wine a staggering 14s.6d (72.5p). The Wimpy Brunch was 4s.9d (24p) and the Wimpy Special Grill 5s.9d (29p).

(Above) Christmas lights, Lord Street, near the corner with Whitechapel, Liverpool, 25 November 1962.

(Opposite Top) Ken Dodd and six-year-old Pamela Clee of Toxteth take a look at the Church Street Christmas lights he had just officially switched on. November 1969.

(Opposite Bottom) Christmas shoppers at Lewis's Department Store, Liverpool, 2 December 1966.

'Mmmm. Now what do I ask Santa for?' Four-year-old Christine McDonald of Kirkdale looks over the goodies on offer. There is a rocking horse at 44/11 (£2.4s.11d), and a bear stuffed with hygienic filling – a snip at 2Gns (£2.2s.0d). 30 November 1962.

Christmas card scene in Clayton Square, Liverpool, 31 December 1962.

The rush is on at the wool counter at Lewis's as the store starts its post-Christmas sale. December 1969.

(Above). Mrs Elizabeth Moore on her stall at St John's Old Market, Liverpool, on 28 February 1964. She had been trading since 1895. (Above right). Sarah Burke, who at what was then the grand old age of 78, pictured selling flowers on the streets of Liverpool in February 1961.

(Above). Former Scottish international and Liverpool goal keeper Tommy Young keeps fit pulling pints in his pub in January 1961. He signed for Liverpool from Hibernian for £9000 in June 1956 and made 127 League and FA Cup appearances during his three seasons with the club. He had a spell at Falkirk as player-manager.

The fire at Henderson's Department Store, Church Street, Liverpool, on Wednesday, 22 June 1960, is seared into the memory of anyone who witnessed it. Henderson's was a high-class store, recently acquired by the House of Fraser chain. Wednesday was half-day closing in Liverpool and Henderson's was one of the few stores that remained open. This particular day was hot and sunny and all the store's doors were wide open.

At around 2.20pm, the store manager was on the third floor when he heard a 'crackling' sound. Looking up he saw a bright flickering from the suspended ceiling and, realising that it was a fire, contacted the store's telephonist to call the Liverpool Fire Brigade. The manager then tackled the fire with an extinguisher.

The first fire appliance was on the scene within three minutes of the LFB being called. A quick appraisal by the senior fire officer present resulted in an immediate call for reinforcements and over the next half hour there were calls for more fire appliances and ambulances.

At 3.05pm, the fire had taken such a hold that firefighters were ordered out of the building. It was not before time as just a few minutes later the central section of the front of the building collapsed. Reinforcements were requested from the Bootle, Birkenhead, Wallasey and South Lancashire Brigades and the demand for water was such that the fireboat *William Gregson* was brought alongside the Pier Head to pump water from the Mersey.

At 5.44pm, the fire was under control though not without loss as eleven people had died. Fireman George Taylor climbed the turntable ladder to rescue several people trapped on a ledge on the fourth floor. As George was climbing, one of the people to the left of the ladder fell. This was Colin Murphy from the Liverpool Ventilation Co who had been at the store working on the first floor. Having left the building, he went back in to switch off the ventilation fans. But by the time he found they were already off, he was trapped on the fourth floor. With others, he climbed out on to an 18inch wide ledge and started to edge toward Timothy White's store. Suddenly there was a rush of smoke and flame from a fourth-floor window. Colin lost his footing, slipped and plunged one hundred feet to the ground, crashing through the store canopy on the way. He died later of injuries.

At the subsequent inquiry it was found that the fire was caused by an electrical fault. It was also found that, for a few minutes, store staff had attempted to fight the fire. There were only two or three extinguishers on each floor and nine had been used with effect. Also, there was no evacuation. However, before we judge by 2017 standards, we must remember this was the norm for the period.

Peter Morton Smith, a junior salesman, attempted to save several people. For his actions and by command of her majesty Queen Elizabeth II, his name was published in the *London Gazette* on 10 March 1961.

These two photographs show the same area of Lime Street on 19 June 1964, and again in February 1969, when the Ravenseft redevelopment was under way.

Kids take advantage of a strike by building workers to get at the sand on the Catholic Cathedral site.

One of the many street parties held around
Merseyside to celebrate the consecration of
Liverpool Metropolitan Cathedral on 14 May 1967.

(Below) The massive sandstone Gothic tower of
the Anglican Cathedral and the modern lantern
tower of the Metropolitan could not be more
different in design yet are separated by only a few
decades in age.

Built on St James's Mount, the foundation stone of the Cathedral Church of Christ in Liverpool was laid by King Edward VII and Queen Alexandra in July 1904, though the building would not be formally completed until 1978, eleven years after the Roman Catholic Metropolitan Cathedral. Our image was taken on 3 November 1967.

For more than fifty years, the Royal Liver Building – standing at 295ft high and often considered to be the UK's first skyscraper - was the tallest building in Liverpool. This came to an end with the topping out of St John's Beacon, a free-standing radio and tower 452ft tall, with a revolving restaurant near the top. These images from the topping out ceremony show how much of the city skyline looked like back then.

The World of Work

The County Class destroyer *HMS Devonshire* glides down the slipway at Cammell Laird on 10 June 1960. Devonshire was the first guided missile destroyer built for the Royal Navy and, at 5440tonnes (6850tonnes full load), she was bigger than some of the navy's cruisers that served during the Second World War. In 1962, she became the first commissioned warship to fire radar controlled Seaslug SAM missiles, designed for use against high altitude targets such as bombers.

The missiles achieved a hit rate of 92% though the main drawback was the ship could only lock on one target at a time. However, as it carried a twin mount, it could fire two Seaslugs at the same target. Short-range anti-aircraft protection was provided by Seacat SAM missiles – designed to replace the 40mm Bofors gun. Her main battery consisted of two twin 4.5inch turrets mounted forward. Other weapons included a pair of 20mm AA guns, two triple 324mm torpedo tubes and a helicopter.

In 1962, British Petroleum ordered a pair of 43,000grt steam turbine tankers: *British Ensign* from Cammell Laird and *British Mariner* from John Brown, Clydebank. With a length of 815ft and a beam of 113ft, these 16knot vessels were, for a short while, the largest vessels in the BP fleet. Our image shows *British Ensign* shortly after being launched.

As well as shipbuilding and refits, Cammell Laird, Birkenhead, undertook heavy engineering contracts. This photograph, taken in the boiler shop in November 1967, shows a 200tonne pressure vessel being lifted onto low loaders.

The ballistic missile submarine *HMS Renown* takes to the water for the first time as she slides into the Mersey on 25 February 1967. The yard also built *HMS Conqueror,* the third boat in the Churchill class of nuclear-powered fleet submarines launched on 28 August 1969, as well as the ballistic missile submarine *HMS Revenge.*

Paddy Neary, National chairman of the Seamen's Reform Movement, is welcomed back to Liverpool following his release from Brixton jail in October 1960. During the summer of 1960, Liverpool's dockers were demanding a cut in hours and an increase in wages, coming out on strike at the beginning of July. Shortly afterwards, many of the city's seafarers walked off their ships over similar demands – a reduction in the working week from 56 to 44hours and an increase in pay of £4 a month.

The seafarers' demand for a reduction in hours was long-standing but their union, the National Union of Seamen (NUS), had been dragging its heels – little or nothing had been done. Liverpool's seafarers lit the blue touch paper by forming the Seamen's Reform Movement (SRM), not only to fight for better conditions but also to reform the NUS, the leaders of which appeared to have a cosy relationship with the ship owners. To make matters worse for both the NUS and the ship owners, seafarers in other ports joined the strike. Stung into action, the NUS negotiated a reduction in the working week to 52hours at sea and 44hours in port. However, this was rejected by the SRM because it offered little as ships spent most of their time a sea. A few weeks after returning to work, the seafarers were back on strike.

Sir Tom Yates, General Secretary of the NUS, branded the leaders of the SRM as 'Communists dedicated to disruption,' and, immediately after the seamen returned to work, the knives came out. Sixteen seamen based in London were arrested and nearly forty more were detained in Montreal. On 13 August, arrest warrants were issued against the Liverpool leaders of the SRM for 'intimidation.'

On 16 August, Merseyside dockers came out for a day in support of the seamen and a march estimated at between 5000-6000 strong made its way in silent protest to the Pier Head. Thanks to the Cunard Shipping Co, Paddy Neary was charged under the antiquated 1894 Merchant Shipping Act for conspiring to incite Cunard seamen to break their contract of employment. On 23 August, he was found guilty in the High Court of contempt of court, a summary conviction, and jailed. This out-of-touch act by the establishment roused a storm of protest with the TUC and Labour calling for demonstrations to take place on Tuesday 30 August. The march through Liverpool was, at the time, the largest ever seen in the city. Mediation took place and common sense eventually won the day. Paddy Neary was released after serving seven weeks.

Liverpool Docks on 16 May 1966, the first day of the national strike called by the National Union of Seamen over demands for a reduction in the working week from 56hours to 40hours. It was the first time since 1911 that the union had called a national strike. By 23 May, some £40million worth of exports were stuck at UK ports and by 1 June some 20,000 seafarers were on strike. Minister of Labour Ray Gunter admitted that working conditions needed modernising but the reduction in hours would – because of overtime payments - breach the government's 3.5% limit on wage rises. Prime Minister Harold Wilson criticised the strikers, claiming the union had been taken over by communists whose sole aim was to bring down his administration. A state of emergency was declared, though the powers were not used, and there was a run on the pound. A cap on food prices was introduced to stop profiteering. Very quickly, UK ports became choked with strike-bound ships. The Royal Navy was authorised to take control of ports and move vessels to free up berths. When the strike came to an end on 1 July, there were 891 immobilised vessels around the UK. (Below). Mersey Area members of the National Union of Seamen vote at a mass meeting on the Pierhead, 16 May 1966.

The seamen's strike is over and the first ship to leave Birkenhead is Blue Funnel Line's *Agapenor*, seen here manoeuvring out of the Alfred Dock aided by tugs. In 1967, *Agapenor* was one of fifteen ships transiting the Suez Canal when war between Israel and Egypt broke out. Fourteen ships were forced to anchor in the Bitter Lakes, whilst the *SS Observer* was cut off in Lake Timsah. Of the four British ships, three were from Liverpool; Blue Funnel Line's *Agapenor* and *Melampus*, and Blue Star Line's *Scottish Star*. The other British vessel was Port Line's *Port Invercargill*. In October 1967, the crews met aboard Melampus and organised the Great Bitter Lakes Association. A cinema was established on Navigation Maritime's *Vassil Levsky*, soccer aboard the *Port Invercargill* and swimming aboard Rederiakiebolaget Transatlantic's *Killara*. During 1968, the crews even held a mini Olympic Games.

Ellerman Lines *City of Pretoria* in the West Float, Birkenhead, 7 May 1966. (Clive Hardy).

Ellerman Lines' 7557grt *City of Brooklyn*, makes a fine sight in Canada Dock, dressed overall on 20 February 1960, to celebrate the birth of Prince Andrew (born 19 February 1960).

Dockers at work loading a ship at Gladstone Dock, 9 August 1965.

Until 1903, buckets were used to unload grain ships. Then a revolution occurred. The resident engineer at the newly opened Central Granary, Millwall Dock, London, had designed and built a pneumatic suction elevator. Grain could now be unloaded in a fraction of the time it took with buckets. This image from December 1962, shows one of the pneumatic suction elevators in action at the Spillers storage silos on the west side of the West Float.

In February 1969, thousands of Merseysiders lined the waterfront, and passengers on the ferry *Mountwood* were crowded on one side, to watch the 209,805dwt tanker *Melo* manoeuvre into the Tranmere oil terminal. Recently completed at the Kawasaki Heavy Industries yard at Sakaide, Japan, Melo, 1067ft long and with a beam of 154ft, belonged to Shell Tankers UK first class of VLCC (very large crude carrier) supertankers.

The 20,000th Ford Escort manufactured at Halewood is loaded at Garston Dock bound for Finland.

(Below) Tranmere oil terminal, Birkenhead, showing the floating berths originally constructed to handle vessels of up to 65,000tonnes and officially opened on 8 June 1960. (Above). The 38,788dwt tanker *Zenatia* alongside is preparing to discharge.

Port Sunlight and Bromborough Dock.

Birkenhead Docks, 27 January 1965.

Some of the first recruits for the new Ford car factory in Halewood undergo training in a hangar at Speke Airport, 2 January 1962. Construction on the 346acre site began in 1961, the plant opening in 1963 to build the Ford Anglia. In 1967 the Anglia was phased out and the plant switched to producing the Ford Escort. The other images on this page were taken on the production line on 23 January 1967.

A Ford Capri on the assembly line at Halewood, October 1963. Car ownership rocketed during the decade – from 5.6million in 1960 to 11.8million in 1965. In 1965, a Morris Minor Traveller cost £583 and a Rover 2000 cost £1298 and, by the end of the Sixties, there was 600 miles of motorways to thrash them on. By 1966, the top-selling car was the Ford Cortina series. The Cortina II sold for £669, the estate version for £724.

(Middle). On 7 June 1968, 187 women sewing machinists at the Ford plant in Dagenham downed tools over sex discrimination in job grading. They were classed as B grade unskilled workers, whilst male colleagues doing the same job – making car-seat covers - were classed as C grade semi-skilled workers. They were soon joined by 195 women machinists working at Halewood. Little did they know it at the time, but it would turn out to be one of the most important strikes in the UK involving women since that of the matchgirls in 1888.

Their actions attracted worldwide attention, especially when Ford's output was brought to a standstill. The women soon found that not only were they fighting Ford, they were fighting the unions. 135 of the Dagenham women were members of the National Union of Vehicle Builders (NUVB) but found little in the way of backing apart from their local district official Fred Blake. The mighty Transport & General Workers Union (T&GWU) refused to back them, though the engineering union at Dagenham backed them on equal pay but not regrading. The women were also ridiculed by male colleagues as well as those sections of the press who clung to the line that they ought to be caring for their families, not out earning pin money.

As the strike entered its second week, Employment Secretary Barbara Castle was despatched by Harold Wilson to help negotiations. It was over tea with her that shop steward Rosie Boland raised the issue of equal pay to which Cartland was sympathetic. After three weeks on strike, they settled for 92per cent of the C grade rate but it would take another sixteen years and another strike to force Ford to regrade them. The strike led directly to the Equal Pay Act 1970 and influenced the fledgling women's movement. Our image shows some of the women from the Halewood plant on their way to T&GWU headquarters for a mass meeting.

In 2010, the story of the strike was told in the film *Made in Dagenham*. Its stars included Sally Hawkins, Bob Hoskins, Miranda Richardson, Geraldine James, Rosamund Pike and Andrea Riseborough. The music was by Billy Bragg and the theme song was sung by former Ford clerk Sandie Shaw. The stage musical premiered in 2014.

(Left) Standard Triumph assembly line at Speke, February 1968. During 1967-68, Harold Wilson's government allocated £225million for road building and introduced legislation governing the use of seat belts, breathalyser tests, and lorry drivers' hours. It also introduced an experimental 70mph speed limit. The Transport Act 1968 also provided funds to local authorities to maintain passenger services if justified on social grounds.

During December 1969, staff at the Sir Alfred
Jones Memorial Hospital, Garston, were hit
by the flu epidemic then sweeping across
Merseyside. With 29 out of 31 nurses off sick,
matron Miss Queenie Graham put out a call for
volunteers to save the hospital from closing.

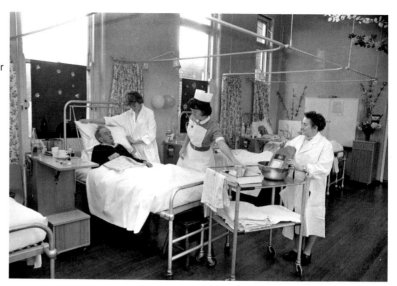

Doctor N Cantrill busily inoculating children
at Kirkby's town centre clinic on 2 May 1961,
following the report of a suspected case of
polio in the area. Receiving a jab is eleven-
year-old Mary Wilson.

It is January 1962 and worried parents
take their children to the Halton Road
Divisional Health Centre, Runcorn, for
smallpox vaccinations. The first indication
that Britain might be facing an outbreak of
smallpox emerged during December 1961
when several people arriving from Pakistan
were suspected of being carriers. On 1
January, one of these people was isolated
in Bradford Fever Hospital. Ten days later
the first case amongst Bradford's population
was confirmed. That same month, smallpox
broke out in the Rhondda – again the carrier
was from Pakistan. A massive vaccination
programme was launched nationwide.

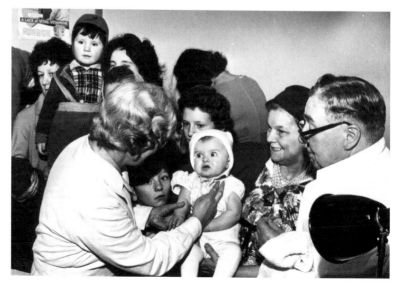

Having pulled a 6.00am to 2.00pm shift packing sugar for Tate & Lyle, it was off to the Corporation laundry to do the washing. Liverpool holds the distinction of having the first public wash-house in the UK thanks to the pioneering work of Kitty Wilkinson, who came to the city in the 1830s. During cholera outbreaks she allowed neighbours to use her hot water to wash their clothes.

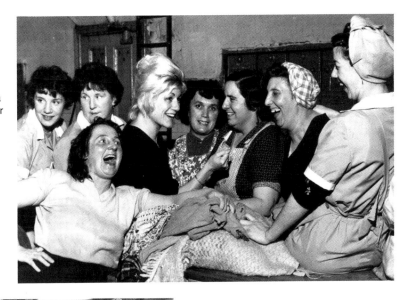

With just five delivery days to go to Christmas, the main sorting office for Merseyside is working flat out. 20 December 1960.

Three of Liverpool's finest on patrol around Kirkby, March 1965.

On the Move?

(Opposite page top). The *Empress of Canada* leaves the Mersey on her maiden voyage. *Empress of Canada* was designed to spend the winter months cruising the Caribbean as a one-class ship. By 1969, air travel was making such inroads into the transatlantic market that CP deployed *Empress of Canada* on year-round cruising. After 121 transatlantic crossings and 82 cruises, she arrived at Liverpool for the last time on 23 November 1971. On 14 December, she sailed out of the Mersey bound for Tilbury to be laid up. With her departure, Liverpool's connection with Canadian Pacific came to an end.

(Opposite page bottom). Built by John Brown & Co, Glasgow, the latest addition to Blue Funnel Line, the 8,262grt *Centaur*, departs Liverpool for Australia via the Suez Canal and Singapore, on 20 January 1964. Costing £1.5million, *Centaur* could carry general and refrigerated cargo, as well as up to 700 cattle or 4,500 sheep. Her high superstructure, which housed accommodation for up to 196 passengers, and tall funnel gave her a distinctive look. She arrived in Sydney on 23 February. Her first voyage out of Australia was as a floating exhibition centre for the Australian Department of Commerce's trade mission to the Far East and Japan.

(Top). One of the ferries heads away from Pier Head. 17 January 1965. (Clive Hardy).

(Middle). *Royal Daffodil II* was the last ferry built for Wallasey Corporation, entering service in 1958. At 609 gross tons, she was licenced to carry 1950 passengers. On 8 September 1967, she ran aground on a sandbank in thick fog, her sixty passengers were taken off by the New Brighton lifeboat and put ashore at the Seacombe landing stage.

(Bottom). A busy scene at Liverpool landing stage during Easter weekend, April 1960, as passengers queue for ferries to New Brighton, Wallasey and Birkenhead.

YOUR CHANCE TO MAKE HISTORY

BOOK YOUR SEAT NOW ON THE WORLD'S FIRST HOVERCOACH

REGULAR DAILY SERVICES BETWEEN WALLASEY AND RHYL

£1 SINGLE   £2 RETURN

20th JULY to 16th SEPTEMBER 1962

THE VICKERS VA-3

operated by

BRITISH UNITED AIRWAYS

FUELS BP OILS

In July 1962, the Wirral was the location for the world's first passenger and mail hovercraft service. Owned by British United Airways and managed by Furness Withy Ship Management Ltd, the Vickers VA3 weighed ten tons and could carry 24 passengers as well as mail at speeds up to 60knots. As the VA3 lacked a skirt, it hovered just eight inches above a solid surface which meant it could only operate in calm weather.

The service, of six return trips a day between Leasowe embankment and Rhyl, commenced on 20 July and was scheduled to operate for two months for experimental purposes. Hoylake had been first choice for the Wirral end of the operation but Leasowe was decided upon as it had a flat beach and would reduce engine noise. However, the service – which proved extremely popular - operated for a total of 36 days as stormy winds, high seas and engine failures put paid to the other 23 days. On Friday 14 September, the day's service was cut short due to the failure of one of the hovercraft's lift engines. Bad weather made it impossible to undertake repairs and, on the following Sunday, the VA3 broke free from its moorings and drifted out to sea. Her duty pilot, Captain Old, who had remained aboard, managed to fire up the propulsion engines and, when the tide receded, brought the hovercraft on to the beach. Unfortunately, VA3 broke free again the following day and had to be rescued by the Rhyl lifeboat. VA3 suffered structural damage and the service was curtailed. Fares were single £1, return £2 (multiply by 20.11 for 2017 comparison).

Mersey Docks & Harbour Board 65-year-old shunt locomotive No.1 newly repainted – including white buffers - pauses during a tour of the dock railway system by members of Liverpool University Transport Society on 8 May 1965. Members of the society were carried in ordinary open goods wagons, old No.1 at one end of the train and a modern diesel shunter at the other. At its height the Mersey Docks & Harbour Board system totalled 104miles of trackwork.
(Courtesy Clive Hardy).

Liverpool's dock railway system connected with British Railways at several locations and shunt engines like the two shown here could often be seen trundling along Dock Road. The peculiar objects attached to the engines' chimneys are baffle plates. Once these engines ran on lines that were underneath the Liverpool Overhead Railway (LOR) and the baffle plates were intended to keep their sulphurous exhausts from polluting the LOR decking above. The baffle plates were not removed after the LOR closed. This image was taken at Bank Hall motive power depot shortly before 51206 was withdrawn from service.
(Courtesy Clive Hardy).

E3100 was one of a batch of fifteen electric locomotives built by English Electric at the Vulcan Foundry, Newton-le-Willows, between 1960-62, for the newly electrified line between Birmingham and the North West. Originally, this loco was to have been geared for working freight trains but instead BR decided to use it as a testbed for silicon rectifiers and transductors. During 1965-66, the firm built sixty more electric locos for BR's West Coast Main Line. One of these, E3173, was experimentally fitted with helical flexi-coil springs on its bogies earning it the nickname Zebedee after the springy character in the TV series *Magic Roundabout*.

Everton pose for the press at Lime Street prior to departing for London and the 1966 FA Cup Final against Sheffield Wednesday. (Below). Keeper Andy Rankin gives the thumbs up as the train departs.

Liverpool Central, 30 March 1965. This is the BR high level station that once had services to Manchester Central, Harwich, Hull and London St Pancras. From 1966, most services were diverted to Lime Street via Hunts Cross Chord and what was left was finally withdrawn in April 1972. The station was demolished the following year.

The time is 7.58pm on 11 August 1968 and 45110 comes to a stand in Lime Street Station - with it comes to an end the use of steam traction by British Rail. 1T57, or the "Fifteen Guinea Special," was a special from Liverpool to Carlisle via Manchester Victoria and back, using four different locomotives in turn during the four legs of the journey. The following day, apart from the narrow-gauge Vale of Rheidol line, BR introduced a steam ban throughout the UK, though one locomotive was exempt. Due to contractual arrangements, the preserved steam locomotive Flying Scotsman could still venture out on to the main line.

One-way traffic comes to Hamilton Square, Birkenhead, on 1 September 1961.

The showpiece of Birkenhead's 1961 Christmas lights was the illuminated traffic island opposite the Grange Hotel.

Home Secretary Roy Jenkins gets behind the wheel of one of the beat patrol cars allocated to Kirkby police station. With him is PC Michael Pacey. May 1966.

By the early 1960s, there were times during the day when the Queensway Tunnel was a choke point, unable to cope with the volume of traffic trying to use it. Here traffic is jammed in to the mouth of St John's Lane. Lime Street Station is in the background.

Football pools magnate Sir John Moores and his Rolls-Royce, 11 January 1968.

Considered by many to be the most popular car of the twentieth century, the Mk I Mini was introduced in 1959 and remained in production until 1967 when it was replaced by the Mk II. Designed by Alec Issigonis, the Mini was light, cheap to run and a steal at £497. Despite its size, Issigonis' radical design resulted in the Mini having more room inside than its predecessor, the Morris Minor. By 1965, more than one million had been sold. The car achieved international fame in 1969 when Minis were the getaway car of choice for Charlie Croker (Michael Caine) and his light-fingered lads in the movie *The Italian Job*.

77-year-old Florrie Ball of Southport takes to the road on her new Yamaha. With her is her insurance agent Arthur Edwards. 11 February 1969.

The new Runcorn - Widnes road bridge under construction. The photograph was taken from the railway bridge. The transporter bridge, with its gondola for carrying vehicles and passenger over the Mersey can be seen on the right. The new bridge was opened by Princess Alexandria on 21 July 1961. For the first time, Runcorn had easy road access to Widnes, Liverpool and beyond. It was said that Runcorn retailers and businesses subsequently enjoyed a ten-fold increase in turnover.

Built in early 1945, De Havilland Mosquito TA634 was used for target towing from 1952 to 1963 when it was purchased by Liverpool Corporation for £720 and flown to Speke. During 1968, the aircraft was restored to air worthiness at Speke – making its first flight on 17 June - to be one of three fully operational Mosquitos used in the movie *Mosquito Squadron*, starring *Man from Uncle* actor David McCallum, Suzanne Neve and Charles Gray. Filming was done at RAF Bovington, TA634 returning to Speke on 16 July 1969. TA634 was donated to the Mosquito Museum, departing Speke by road on 29 September 1970. Our image shows TA634 taking off for RAF Bovington.

In July 1967, the Commonwealth Curtain Company decided to send 28 members of staff from its Kirkby Industrial Estate site to the company's plant at Montreal, Canada. The visit would last a week and there would be some sightseeing.

Air hostess Paddy Clinch of Dublin presents Liverpool skipper Ron Yeats with a lucky leprechaun as the team prepare to board their flight to Sweden for the round one, first leg, Fairs Cup game against Malmo. The game was played on 19 September 1967, centre forward Tony Hateley scoring both goals in the 2-0 win.

Firefighters at Speke Airport try out the latest addition to the fleet – a new fire-fighting and rescue tender costing £15,000. Whilst the test was under way just off the main runway and black smoke and flames billowed skywards, a 50-seater airliner happened to be coming into land. The pilot calmly reassured the passengers that it was just an exercise.

Rock, Pop and Merseybeat

Promoted by Larry Parnes, *The Rock 'n Trad Spectacular – The New Noise of 1960* was a massive forty-five venue tour starring 'Billy Fury and his company of 50.' Among the company were Joe Brown, Tommy Bruce, Nelson Keene, the Vernons Girls, and Georgie Fame. Davy Jones (later of the Monkees) and Vince Eager were amongst performers who appeared at some venues but not others. The show kicked off at the Adelphi, Slough, on 24 September and played the Manchester Free Trade Hall on 7 October. The show came to Liverpool for a week's residency, opening on 7 November, returning to Manchester on 14 November for a week at the Manchester Hippodrome. The show was such a hit that additional venues had to be arranged and it ended with a one-week residency at the Newcastle Empire commencing 5 December. Among the support acts was a young pianist by the name of Georgie Fame – real name Clive Powell. Born in Leigh, Powell's undoubted talent was evident by the time he was sixteen. Following an audition, he was signed by Larry Parnes as a backing musician and changed his name. He was one of Parnes' musicians chosen by Billy Fury to form his personal backing group The Blue Flames. At the end of 1961, there was some sort of disagreement between Fury and the Blue Flames, resulting in them parting company. They became Georgie Fame and The Blue Flames.

Billy Fury.

Georgie Fame.

The Vernons Girls at the Royal Albert Hall on 15 September 1963. The show, in aid of the Printers Pension Corporation, also included the Rolling Stones – who opened - the Viscounts, Kenny Lynch, Susan Maughan, Shane Fenton and the Fentones, Clinton Ford, The Lorne Gibson Trio, Arthur Greenslade and The G-Men, Helen Shapiro and Karl Denver. Top of the bill were The Beatles who closed the show.

Originally, the Vernons Girls had been formed in the 1950s as a sixteen-strong choir by workers at Vernons Pools, but by the early 1960s it was down to five members, then three. Signed to Decca, they released covers of US hits including: *Lover Please/You Know What I Mean*, which reached No.16 during its twenty weeks run in the UK singles charts. Their next single to chart, *Loco-Motion*, reached No.47 and two further singles went on to reach the top fifty; *Funny All Over* made it to No.31 and *Do The Bird* got to No.44. There then followed a run of five singles that failed to chart, including We Love The Beatles – which charted in the US. The girls enjoyed another US hit, *We Love You Beatles*, released under the name The Carefrees.

Though their own chart success was limited, the Vernons Girls provided the female backing on many Decca hit singles, including Billy Fury's *Maybe Tomorrow*. The girls also appeared in the Billy Fury movie, *Play it Cool*. In 1964, Jean Owen, Frances Lea and Maureen Kennedy appeared in the TV special *Around with the Beatles*. The Vernons Girls disbanded in 1964.

Some of the Vernons Girls married into the business. Vicky Haseman married Joe Brown. Joyce Smith married Marty Wilde. Maureen Kennedy married comedian Mike Hope. Maggie Stredder married writer Roy Tuvey. Lynn Cornell married drummer Andy White, who replaced Ringo Starr on the Beatles first single *Love Me Do* and played drums on *P.S. I Love You*. He also played on Billy Fury's first album and performed with Herman's Hermits and Chuck Berry.

The Three Bells were formed in Liverpool by Jean Bell and her identical twin sisters Sue and Carol. They were signed by Pye in 1960 but were dropped when their singles *Steady Date* and *Melody of Love* failed to chart. The girls carried on and, in 1964, were offered a contract by Columbia and released a cover of *Softly in the Night* by US girl group The Cookies. The B side, *He Dosen't Love Me*, was also recorded by another Liverpool girl group The Breakaways. Our image dates from June 1965, following Columbia's insistence the girls adopt blonde bouffant hair styles in time for the July release of their second single, *Someone to Love*, which was written by the girls themselves. Once again, they failed to chart and Columbia pulled out the stops to get the girls as much publicity as possible prior to the release of their third single *Cry No More*. The plan failed, the record tanked, and Columbia dropped them.

Determined to carry on, they reinvented themselves becoming the Satin Bells and, lo and behold, were signed by Pye. During 1968, they released two singles, the soul number *Baby, You're So Right For Me* and a cover of French recording star France Gall's *Dady da da*, under the anglicised title of *Da-di-da-da*. Both failed to chart and, for the second time, Pye sent the girls on their way.

In 1969, they managed to secure a contract with Decca, releasing a cover of Martha Reeves and The Vandellas' *Sweet Darlin'* followed by *Power of Love*. Again, both UK releases failed to chart, and they were let go. They released several singles in Germany, the Netherlands and Spain and enjoyed more success on the Continent than home. The girls' last release in the UK was *The Belle Telephone Song* for CBS. It too failed to chart. The main problem was that the white soul the girls loved to record and perform failed to attract many UK soul fans as recordings by original US artists were readily available. However, *Someone to Love* later became a mod classic.

The Escorts on stage at the Cavern. Formed in 1962 by three friends from the Morrison School for Boys, Allerton – Mike Gregory, John Kinrade and Terry Sylvester - they proved to be talented musicians. In 1963, readers of *Mersey Beat Magazine* voted them the ninth most popular group in Liverpool. They made their first appearance at the Cavern on New Year's Eve 1963 and were soon filling the lunchtime slot on a regular basis. In those days, the group booked for the lunchtime session was also booked to appear the same evening with two or three other groups. After lunch time, Cavern manager Ray McFall would hand over the keys to the club so the boys could leave their kit set up and come back and rehearse before the club opened in the evening.

Our image shows, left to right, John Kinrade, Mike Gregory (bass) and Terry Sylvester (guitar and lead vocals). Hidden at the back on drums is Pete Clarke. The Escorts' first single was a cover of Larry Williams' *Dizzy Miss Lizzy*, released in April 1964, some sixteen months before The Beatles released their version. Their second single, *The One to Cry*, was released two months later and on 2 July it entered the UK charts, making it to No.49. During 1965, two more singles, including a cover of The Drifters, *I Don't Want to go on Without You*, were released but failed to chart. In January 1966, they released a good cover of *Let it be Me*, a song dating from 1955 and originally composed in French as *Je t'appartiens*. The English version was first recorded by the Everly Brothers. Surprisingly, it too failed to chart. Terry Sylvester left to join The Swinging Blue Jeans and was replaced in the Escorts by Frank Townsend. The group made one more record, *From Head to Toe*, on which Paul McCartney played tambourine. It too failed and the group split, with Mike Gregory joining the Swinging Blue Jeans and Pete Clarke becoming the in-house session drummer at Apple Records. John Kinrade gave up the music business. In January 1969, Terry Sylvester joined the Hollies following Graham Nash's departure.

Terry Sylvester was convinced that if the Escorts had had Brian Epstein as manager, they would have made hit records. Our second image shows Terry (second from left) playing with the Hollies on Top of the Pops, May 1969.

Cilla Black photographed by *Echo* photographer Gordon Whiting at the Cavern Club c1963. Priscilla Maria Veronica White was determined to be a singer and her first step was to take a part-time job as a cloakroom attendant at the Cavern Club. Taking to the stage whenever the opportunity presented itself, Cilla's singing impressed local promoter Sam Leach who booked her for the Casanova Club under the name Swinging Cilla. Cilla also made appearances with Kingsize Taylor and the Dominoes and Rory Storm and the Hurricanes. Cilla is said to have taken the stage name Black after Bill Harry of *Mersey Beat* magazine referred to her as such in the first edition.

Cilla, backed by The Beatles, auditioned for Brian Epstein but unfortunately things did not work out – almost certainly due to the songs being played to suit The Beatles' vocal range rather than hers. However, it all turned out well in the end. Epstein heard Cilla performing at the Blue Angel Jazz Club and signed her. She was his only female client.

Cilla Black and Gerry Marsden on the dance floor at the Cavern. Cilla Black would become one of the UK's favourite female vocalists, but when *Echo* photographer Gordon Whiting took this image she was still relatively unknown outside Liverpool. Her second single *Anyone Who Had A Heart* had just entered the charts and, during its seventeen-week run, would reach No.1, overlapping with her third release, *You're My World*, which would also go to No.1. Though these two would be her only No.1 UK hits, Cilla enjoyed 1960s Top 10 singles hits with *It's For You* (No.7), *You've Lost That Lovin' Feelin'* (No.2), *Love's Just A Broken Heart* (No.5), *Alfie* (No.9), *Don't Answer Me* (No.6), *Step Inside Love* (No.8), *Surround Yourself With Sorrow* (No.3) and *Conversations* (No.7). During the 1960s, Cilla also had three Top Ten albums, *Cilla* (No.5), *Cilla Sings A Rainbow* (No.4) and *Sher-oo* (No.7).

Ringo Starr's original group, Rory Storm and the Hurricanes led by singer Rory Storm (Alan Caldwell), never quite made it to the top. As with many Merseyside groups of the late 1950s, they played skiffle with a little jazz thrown in for luck. However, this is the band that brought rock 'n' roll to the Cavern Club. At the time, the Cavern was a jazz club but at one gig the boys played their version of Lonnie Donegan's 1957 No.1 skiffle hit *Cumberland Gap*, only to follow it up with Jerry Lee Lewis's rock 'n' roll smash *Whole Lotta Shakin' Goin' On*. It was all too much for the jazz fans. Change was thrown and the band booed off stage. Cavern manager Ray MacFall went ballistic and fined the boys part of their fee – which they more than made up for by picking up the coins.

In 1963 they released a single, *Dr Feel Good/I Can Tell* but it failed to chart and with it went the chance of a decent recording contract. The group disbanded in 1967 following the death of lead guitarist Ty O'Brien. Having collapsed on stage, he later died of complications following an operation. Our image dates from c1965. Left to right, bass guitarist Wally Eymond, rhythm guitarist Johnny Byrne, vocalist Alan Caldwell, lead guitarist Ty O'Brien and drummer Jimmy Tushingham.

(Opposite page top), Gerry and the Pacemakers on *Thank Your Lucky Stars* in March 1964, performing their latest single *Don't Let the Sun Catch You Crying*. Like many Merseyside groups, Gerry and the Pacemakers cut their teeth on the German beat club scene. They were the second group signed by Brian Epstein and their first single, *How Do You Do It*, went on to become a No.1 hit. Two months later they were at the top again with *I Like It* and, before 1963 was out, had achieved their third straight No.1 with *You'll Never Walk Alone*. In 1963, they also released the album *How Do You Like It?* It reached No.2 during a 28-week run in the charts.

During 1964, they released four singles. *I'm the One* made it to No.2, *Don't Let the Sun Catch You Crying* (No.6), *It's Gonna Be All Right* (No.24) and *Ferry 'Cross the Mersey* (No.8). Their 1965 single releases were *I'll Be There* (No.15) and *Walk Hand In Hand* (No.29).

In 1967 Gerry went solo, concentrating on cabaret work. In 1985, an all-star charity recording of *You'll Never Walk Alone*, in aid of victims of the Bradford City Football Club fire, became a UK No.1 hit. Similarly, the charity recording of *Ferry 'Cross the Mersey*, in aid of Hillsborough, also reached No.1.

Our second image opposite shows Gerry leading the Pacemakers at the IPC *New Musical Express* pop concert at the Empire Pool, Wembley, April 1964.

(Top). Originally formed as a skiffle group by John McNally and Mike Pender, the Searchers' first single for Pye Records, *Sweets for My Sweet*, featuring Tony Jackson as lead vocalist, entered the UK charts on 27 June 1963. It reached No.1 during its sixteen-week run. The group's R&B influenced album *Meet the Searchers* remained in the charts for forty-four weeks, during which time it reached No.2. The album was altered for the US market with the inclusion of *Needles and Pins*. Released there during 1964, it reached No.22 in the US album charts.

Capitalising on the group's success, Phillips Records rushed out an old recording of a cover of Brenda Lee's hit, *Sweet Nuthins*. It only just climbed into the Top 50 Chart, then sank without trace after just two weeks. However, they returned to form with *Sugar and Spice*, which charted on 24 October 1963 and went to No.2.

The Searchers proved astute at covering US hits including *Needles and Pins* and Jackie de Shannon's *When You Walk in the Room*. Our image shows the Searchers line-up as many of us remember it. Left to right: John McNally, Chris Curtis, Tony Jackson and Mike Pender. Tony Jackson was later replaced by Frank Allen.

(Middle). In 1960, Tony Crane and Billy Kinsley formed a group called the Mavericks. A couple of years later, they were casting around for a new name and approached Bill Harry, owner of the *Mersey Beat* magazine for permission to use the name The Mersey Beats. Signed to Fontana and under the name The Merseybeats, they had a No.24 hit with *It's Love That Really Counts*. The Merseybeats were the third group to sign with Brian Epstein but the partnership did not last long. During 1964, the group had four Top 50 singles and a Top 20 album, the highest of which was the single *I Think of You*, which reached No.5 during its seventeen-week run in the charts. Billy Kinsley left to form his own group The Kinsleys. He was replaced by Johnny Gustafsson (later of Roxy Music) but rejoined some months later when Gustafsson was sacked. Their last Top 50 single was *I Stand Accused* which reached No.38 during January 1965. The Merseybeats disbanded in 1966, Tony Crane and Billy Kinsley forming a duet, the Merseys, backed by the Fruit Eating Bears who were unique at the time in having two drummers. As the Merseys, they had a No.4 hit with a cover of the McCoys' *Sorrow*. Our images are of the Kinsleys at the Cavern, featuring Denny Alexandra, Dave Percy and Billy Kinsley with Dave Preston on drums.

(Bottom). The Swinging Blue Jeans pictured in January 1964, their latest single *Hippy Hippy Shake* having entered the UK singles chart on 12 December 1963. It would remain in the Top 50 for seventeen weeks and, on 29 January, it peaked at No.2. On 11 March 1964, their single *Good Golly Miss Molly* entered the charts and reached No.11. Three months later, they enjoyed their second Top Ten hit with *You're No Good*. Their last UK hit single was *Don't Make Me Over*, which reached No.31 in early 1966.

Lunch-time audience at the Cavern, December 1963.

The Cavern Club, February 1965. By July 1965, the Cavern was in financial trouble. Manager Ray McFall was able to call on the services of twenty-five bands who gave their services free of charge during a twelve-hour non-stop session to help the club survive.

(Bottom). The all-Merseyside line up for *Thank Your Lucky Stars* on 15 December 1963. Left to right: Billy J Kramer and The Dakotas, The Beatles, Cilla Black and The Searchers. Between them they had notched up five No.1 and three No.2 hit singles as well as a No.4. In the album charts, *Listen to Billy J Kramer* had reached No.11, The Beatles *Please, Please, Me* and *With The Beatles* had both reached No.1 and would remain in the album chart for 70 and 51 weeks respectively. The Searchers had had album success with *Meet the Searchers* (No.2) and *Sugar and Spice* (No.5). Though Cilla's only chart success had been *Love of the Loved*, which had reached No.35 in the singles chart, she would enjoy two No.1 hit singles during 1964.

The Beatles photographed at ABC TV studio, Aston Cross, Birmingham, for the all-Merseyside edition of *Thank Your Lucky Stars* on 15 December 1963.

Fans queue in the rain outside the Majestic Ballroom, Birkenhead, for tickets to see the Beatles. 17 April 1963.

(Below). Just a few of the 11000 fans queueing on 24 November 1963, for tickets to the Beatles Christmas concert at the Liverpool Empire. The queue stretched an estimated three-quarters of a mile.

(Opposite page bottom). The was a period when, if The Beatles had looked over their shoulders to see who was coming up to challenge them, it would not have been the Rolling Stones, but The Dave Clark Five. Originally, they were a backing group for north London singer Stan Saxon but Stan was not the man and the group went their separate way. They followed the usual early 60s route of recording covers but when Brian Poole and the Tremeloes' cover of *Do You Love Me* beat theirs into the charts, the boys decided to write their own stuff. Their first release was the foot-stomping *Glad All Over* which knocked the Beatles' *I Want To Hold Your Hand* off the top spot. They followed with the even greater foot stomper *Bits And Pieces*. The Dave Clarke Five were canny in that they looked after their own management, allowing them flexibility of when and where to perform.

(Opposite page top). The Rolling Stones at the Tower Ballroom, New Brighton, on 10 August 1964. The same day, Liverpool City Magistrates Court had fined Jagger £32 for speeding and driving without a licence or insurance.

(Right). Pete Best, former Beatles drummer who was sacked and replaced by Ringo Starr, seen here at his home in Hymans Green, Liverpool.

(Top). Jamaican-born singer Millie Small rehearsing her bluebeat hit *My Boy Lollipop* for BBC's *Top of the Pops* at the Dickenson Road Studios, Rusholme, Manchester. Millie's record was released in March 1964 and, by the week ending 7 May, it was at No.2 in the UK charts. Despite selling 600,000 copies, any hopes Millie had of dislodging *Don't Throw Your Love Away* by the Searchers from top position were dashed when fifth placed *Juliet* by The Four Pennies went to No.1 during the week ending 21 May. Millie was the first performer in British pop history to have a hit with a bluebeat record. She released two more singles in the UK, *Sweet William*, which charted on 25 June 1964 and reached No.30 and *Bloodshot Eyes*, which charted on 11 November 1965 and reached No.48.

(Right). The Scaffold – John Gorman, Roger McGough and Mike McGear - photographed on 10 March 1969. During the late 1960s, they had four hit singles, two of which reached the UK Top Ten. On 22 November 1968, *Thank U Very Much* entered the charts, climbing to No.4 during a twelve-week run. The following year, *Do You Remember* reached No.34, whilst *Lily the Pink* made it all the way to the top, staying in the charts for 24 weeks. Their only other hit of the 1960s was *Gin Gan Goolie*, which charted on 1 November 1969 and reached No.38. In 1974, the group had a number No.7 hit with *Liverpool Lou*. Mike McGear's single *Leave It* charted on 5 October 1974 and, during its four-week run, reached No.36.

Liverpool's oldest independent charity, the Liverpool Food Association, was formed in 1893 to provide meals to both the bedridden who had no means of financial support and to starving children around Liverpool, Everton and Bootle. The establishment of the Welfare State in 1948 enabled the charity – now known as the League of Welldoers - to provide other services including offering days out during the summer months. Our images show a pensioners' day out at New Brighton in July 1964.

(Opposite page, top left). Liverpool Playhouse wardrobe mistress Marion Agar (right) assisting dressmaker May Finch with one of the period costumes to be used in a production of *Candida*, October 1960. The image at the bottom of the page shows the new extension shortly after its completion in 1968.

(Opposite page, top right). Anthony Hopkins (left) and Michael Reid in a scene from *The Quare Fellow* at The Playhouse Theatre, Liverpool, in September 1964. Written by Brendan Behan, the title was taken from a Hiberno-English pronunciation of queer, meaning strange or unusual. The play is set in Mountjoy Prison, Dublin, the day before the Quare Fellow is due to be executed, though Behan does not tell us for what crime. Also, the Quare Fellow never appears in the play. The play is a comedy/drama though it gets much darker in the second half as the time for the execution gets ever nearer. Behan had died about six months prior to this production. He collapsed in the Harbour Lights bar, Dublin, on 20 March 1964. At his funeral, he was given an IRA guard of honour.

(Top right). It is October 1965 and Sergeant Bill Davies of the Scots Guards covers his eyes in despair as actor William Ellis once again finds it impossible to keep in step. Sergeant Davies had the unenviable task of drilling actors Brian Miller, William Ellis, Graham Cory, Steven Berkoff, Warren Clarke, Tony Colegate and Bill Kendrick for their roles in *The Long and the Short and the Tall* at Liverpool Playhouse.

(Middle). Written and devised by Troy Kennedy Martin, the BBC crime soap *Z Cars* aired for the first time on 2 January 1962. Set in the fictional northern town of Newtown, each episode ran for 25minutes, following the trials and tribulations of Z Division police station staff and the crews of patrol cars Z-Victor 1 and Z-Victor 2. Martin based Newtown on Kirkby – Merseyside's largest overspill estate where the population had rocketed from 3078 in 1951 to 52,088 in 1961, the result of 10,000 new homes being built there. Martin came up with Z Division having listened in to Lancashire Constabulary radio traffic and the call signs used. Lancashire was divided into divisions, each allocated a letter from the alphabet – B Division was Lancaster etc. As there was no Z Division, Martin was free to use it.

Location filming was done around Liverpool and Kirkby and later around Ruislip in Middlesex. The show's northern setting helped its popularity as, at the time, most output was London-centric: even the tune was based on the Liverpudlian folk song *Johnny Todd*.

Our image shows Brian Blessed – who played Fancy Smith - and Terence Edmund (PC Sweet) toss a coin to see who pays for the tea during a break in filming.

(Bottom). The stars of BBC TV comedy series *Till Death Us Do Part* - Warren Mitchell, who played Hammers loving, right-wing cockney bigot Alf Garnett and Tony Booth, who played his left-wing, Reds supporting, Scouser son-in-law Mike Rawlins - pictured at Anfield on 7 January 1967, during the Liverpool v West Ham United match. As this was a real game, the scriptwriters had to develop storylines for either a Liverpool or West Ham win. Liverpool did not disappoint. Winger Peter Thompson scored both goals in the 2-0 win. In real life, Warren Mitchell was a Labour voter and allegedly a Spurs supporter.

Ken Dodd pictured during rehearsals for his new children's show at the BBC Dickenson Road Studios, Manchester, November 1968.

Ken Dodd plays snooker at Knotty Ash Community Centre, where he challenged the Lord Mayor of Liverpool (Mrs Ethel Wormald) to a game. The comedian, singer-songwriter and actor was identified by his unruly hair, protruding teeth and red, white and blue tickling stick. For several decades he was one of the few performers guaranteed to pack a theatre and was renowned for running over time.

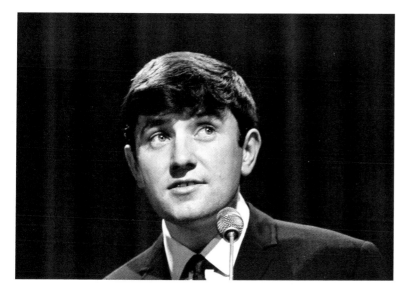

Comedian Jimmy Tarbuck rehearsing, October 1963.

Actor and musician Bill Kenwright played Gordon Clegg in *Coronation Street*. In August 1967, Columbia Records released Bill Kenwright and the Runaways' cover of Chris Clark's Motown hit *I Want to Go Back There Again*. It failed to chart. In fact, it is alleged by some to have been one of the worst records ever played on the Northern Soul circuit. Bill moved to MGM Records and in July 1968 released a solo single *Love's Black and White*. Our photograph shows Bill posing outside the Rovers Return set on 23 July 1968, following an announcement that he would be singing his new song on the programme.

Blue Peter is the longest-running children's TV programme and this picture featuring Peter Purves and John Noakes was taken on 8 December 1969, just four days after the launch of the programme's Christmas appeal for unwanted toy cars. These were to be sold for scrap, the money being used to buy four buses and other equipment to provide transport for old people in the UK. The origins of the programme go back to 16 October 1958, when *Children's Television Club* was aired for the first time.

The 15-minute programme was broadcast from the Wallasey Corporation ferry *Royal Iris* and featured Judith Chalmers as the presenter. It was networked around the UK by BBC Manchester. Though transmitted just once a month, Owen Reed, head of BBC Children's Television, was so impressed with the programme and its content that he negotiated its move to the Television Centre, London. He was also involved in changing the programme's name to *Blue Peter*.

We'll give it five. The Beatles appear on *Juke Box Jury*, 7 December 1963.

On set at the Locarno Ballroom for the movie *Ferry 'Cross the Mersey*, starring Gerry and the Pacemakers, are Cilla Black and The Fourmost. During filming, a real fight broke out and the production company Subafilms were so impressed with it that they kept it in the movie. The film was released in the UK on 13 December 1964, and in the US on 19 February 1965.

Liverpool-born actress Rita Tushingham made her big screen debut in 1961 in the movie *A Taste of Honey*, for which she won a BAFTA and the best actress award at Cannes. Written by Salford playwright Shelagh Delaney, *A Taste of Honey* is a gritty drama that approached the taboos of the day – unmarried mothers, race and homosexuality - head on. Some location filming was done on the Manchester Ship Canal aboard the Manchester Liners' vessel *Manchester Shipper*.

One of the new breed of northern actors who refused to lose their accents, she was a popular choice for films about working class life. In 1964 she starred in a screen adaptation of Edna O'Brien's classic novel *Girl with Green Eyes* as well as in *The Leather Boys* – the story of a working-class woman married to a biker. The following year she starred in *The Knack…and How to Get It* and had a part in the international blockbuster *Dr Zhivago*. This photograph was taken on set during filming for *A Taste of Honey*.

Crowd scene from Friday 10 July 1964. Four days earlier The Beatles' movie *A Hard Day's Night* had premiered in London and the Odeon Cinema, Liverpool, had rightly been chosen as the venue for its northern equivalent. They flew from London to Speke Airport, where at least 3000 fans were waiting and were then driven by police motorcade to Liverpool Town Hall. An estimated 200,000 people lined the route. At the Town Hall, the Lord Mayor, Alderman Louis Caplan, gave each of the boys a set of keys to the city.

The Beatles left the Town Hall at 9pm for the Odeon Cinema. Bessie Braddock MP said. "They are a credit to the city. Juvenile delinquency would be almost non-existent if other boys took a leaf from the Beatles."

The Beatles on stage.

Girls scream as The Beatles perform prior to the premier of *A Hard Day's Night*.

Everton FC

Everton left back Mick Meagan and keeper Albert Dunlop clear a Fulham attack during the last game of the 1962-63 season. Dunlop had joined Everton in 1949, though he did not make his League debut until 20 October 1956, when he replaced Jimmy O'Neill for the home game against Manchester United. After thirteen games that season, Everton had managed to scramble to the dizzy heights of eighteenth in Division One, though for much of September they had occupied one of the relegation places.

Everton beat United 5-2 and Dunlop became first choice keeper until the arrival of Gordon West from Blackpool in March 1962, for what was then a record fee for a goalkeeper of £27,000. Dunlop played in the last four League fixtures of the 1962-63 season – against West Ham United, Bolton Wanderers, West Bromwich Albion and Fulham.

Roy Vernon scores one of his three goals during the 4-1 win over Fulham on 11 May 1963. Everton had spent the entire season bouncing around in one or other of the top three positions, with Spurs and Burnley presenting constant threats to their title ambitions. It was not an easy season. The big freeze over December and January caused chaos with League and cup fixtures. Everton played Sheffield Wednesday on 20 December 1962 and the next League fixture they played was against Leicester City on 12 February 1963. The delay slightly affected form but on 20 April they jumped from third to first following a 1-0 home win against Spurs. Four days later, they drew at home to Arsenal 1-1 and three days after were away to the Hammers whom they beat 2-1. The last three games – against Bolton Wanderers, West Bromwich Albion and Fulham - ended in 1-0, 4-0 and 4-1 victories respectively, though the backlog meant Everton could not be sure of the Championship until their very last game.

The lads celebrate taking the Championship. Everton's 61 points was a club record and winning the title gave them entry to the European Cup.

Everton entered European cup competition for the first time during the 1962-63 season when they played and lost to Dunfermline in Round One of the Inter-Cities Fairs' Cup. Winning the 1962-63 title gave Everton entry to the 1963-64 European Cup where they drew the mighty Inter Milan in Round One.

Apart from the finals which were played at neutral grounds, the rounds in European cup competitions were played over two legs so each side benefited from home advantage. Our image is from the first leg played at Goodison on 18 September 1963 and shows Denis Stevens attempting to avoid Inter keeper Guiliano Sarti. The game ended 0-0. The second leg in Milan on 25 September attracted 90,000 fans. Inter went through to Round Two after winning 1-0.

Colin Harvey celebrates scoring a goal on his derby debut, the third in the 4-0 win at Anfield, 19 September 1964.

(Bottom). 3.39pm on 7 November 1964, was the moment of shame for British football when referee Ken Stokes ordered both sides off the field at Goodison Park where Everton were facing First Division newcomers Leeds United. Whether it was justified or not, Leeds had arrived in the First Division with a reputation for being a dirty side and, by the time Everton left-back Sandy Brown was sent off in the fourth minute for throwing a punch at Johnny Giles, there had already been several heavy tackles. Later, in the dressing room, Brown showed Stokes the six-inch-long graze on his stomach.

League president Joe Richards said he would press for a full inquiry with the FA into football violence at the next League management committee meeting on 17 November. Richards was convinced the bonus scheme was a major cause in the rise of dirty play on the field. 'There has got to be an investigation because the game is getting a bad image. The loss of a point or a goal can mean the loss of a place in the table and with it the loss of several pounds out of the pay packet.' Richards was also concerned how the tenure of managers was changing. 'If a manager loses three games he is in trouble. Winning has become far removed from the manner of winning.'

The game ended 0-1 to Leeds.

The League management committee decided that no League ground should be closed because of the conduct of visiting fans but players found guilty of misconduct could face stiffer punishments. Referees should receive the full backing of the FA by imposing hefty suspensions on guilty players.

Everton's graceful, flowing, sometimes virtuoso forward Alex Young is 'hurried' by none other than Chelsea's Ron 'Chopper' Harris, during the 11 September 1965 fixture at Stamford Bridge. Though Derek Temple scored one for Everton, Chelsea scored three. Chelsea finished the season in fifth place. Liverpool were champions and Everton mid table in eleventh place.

(Bottom). Keeper Andy Rankin spent ten years at Goodison, yet despite his talent he made only 104 senior appearances. This image from the 1965-66 season, shows him pulling off a diving save to deny Leeds United's Jimmy Greenhoff a goal at Elland Road on 16 April 1966. It was Rankin's first senior appearance since the 3-0 defeat at West Ham on 27 November 1965. In 1971, he moved to Watford for £20,000.

"Can you see me, mother?" For Everton, the road to Wembley for the 1966 final against Sheffield Wednesday had not been plain sailing. Though the Fourth Round tie against non-League Bedford Town and the Fifth Round home fixture against Coventry City had both ended in 3-0 victories, Manchester City proved to be a tougher nut to crack. It took Everton two replays to go through 0-2. With the Semi-Final at home to Manchester United ending 1-0, Everton became the first team since Bury in 1903 to reach an FA Cup Final without conceding a goal. (Below). HRH Princess Margaret meets the Everton players before the match.

1966 FA Cup Final. With left-back Ray Wilson guarding his goal line, keeper Brian West punches clear of John Fantham and Jim McCalliog. Sheffield Wednesday went ahead in the fourth minute when Jim McCalliog scored. After the break, they went 2-0 up in the 57th minute thanks to David Ford. However, Owls' fans were still celebrating when two minutes later Mike Trebilcock made it 2-1. Five minutes later Trebilcock equalised. In the 74th minute, Owls' left-half Gerry Young made a mess of a tackle allowing Derek Temple to make off with the ball and slot it past Ron Springett, making it 3-2.

1966 FA Cup Final. Mike Trebilcock's equaliser proved too much for Toffee's fan Eddie Kavanagh, who celebrated by mounting a solo pitch invasion. There then followed what has been described as a Keystone Cops-style chase across the pitch with Eddie expertly dodging the rozzers, though he managed to lose his jacket in the process. Everton's Brian Harris joined in the hilarity by donning the helmet of one of the floored coppers.

Cup celebrations. Everton were the first side since Blackpool in 1953 to come back from being two goals down to win in normal time. By the same token, Sheffield Wednesday became the only side to throw away a two goal lead and lose in normal time whilst fielding a full side.

Everton and the FA Cup trophy leave Allerton station for St Georges Hall in Liverpool city centre.

(Above). Signed from Blackpool in August 1966, Alan Ball commanded what was then the British record fee for a midfielder of £110,000. After making 249 senior League and cup appearances for Everton, he moved to Arsenal in 1971 for another record fee of £220,000.

(Above left). Thanks to the patronage of millionaire supporter John Moores, Everton manager Johnny Carey was able to bring young talent to Goodison. Roy Vernon from Blackburn Rovers, Billy Bingham from Luton Town, Alex Young from Hearts and, pictured here, Jimmy Gabriel from Dundee. At £30,000, Gabriel's fee in March 1960 was, at the time, one of the highest ever paid for a teenager. He made his League debut against West Ham on 5 March 1960 and went on to make more than 300 senior appearances before joining Southampton in 1967.

(Left). Howard Kendall poses during a training session in July 1969, prior to what would prove to be another title winning season. That the club was never out of the top three throughout the campaign is due, in no uncertain terms to their midfield trio of Kendall, Alan Ball and Colin Harvey. Having been signed from Preston North End for £80,000 in March 1967, Kendall spent seven years at Goodison, making a total of 272 senior appearances in League and cup games and scoring 29 goals.

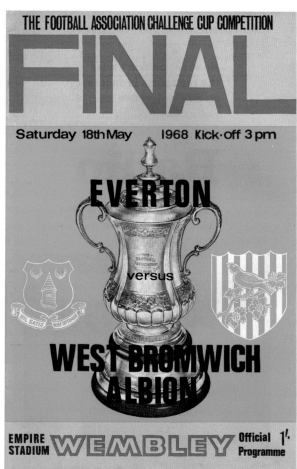

THE FOOTBALL ASSOCIATION CHALLENGE CUP COMPETITION

FINAL

Saturday 18th May   1968 Kick-off 3 pm

EVERTON

versus

WEST BROMWICH ALBION

EMPIRE STADIUM WEMBLEY

Official Programme 1/-

On paper, many would have said that Everton were firm favourites to win the 1968 FA Cup. They had, after all, done the League double over West Bromwich, beating them 2-1 at Goodison on 24 October 1967 and then hammering them 2-6 at the Hawthorns on 16 March 1968. The clubs' road to Wembley could not have been more different. For West Bromwich Albion, it had not been the easiest of competitions. Even Third Division Colchester had taken them to a replay and it took two replays to get past Liverpool. The only game that ended after 90 minutes had been their Semi-Final against Birmingham City. However, the Baggies' League form since their 2-6 hammering had improved. They had beaten Leicester City 3-2, Newcastle United 2-0, West Ham 3-1 and Manchester United 6-3. They had also drawn against Sunderland (twice), Burnley, Newcastle United and Sheffield Wednesday and lost only two fixtures – against Leeds United and Arsenal.

Everton's FA Cup campaign had straightforward, having beaten Southport, Carlisle United, Tranmere Rovers, Leicester City and Leeds United without recourse to replays. This was the first final to be televised in colour, both teams wearing their away strips, Everton donning amber shirts and blue shorts.

In the image above, John Hurst moves in to block a shot by West Brom's Tony Brown and, in the lower image, John Kaye and Joe Royle battle it out for possession. The soggy, slippery pitch did not help. This was not going to be one of the greatest finals, as both sides built up possession only to peter out against solid defences. As the players went off at half time, sections of the crowd could be heard chanting "We want football." Albion's Dennis Clarke came on for injured John Kaye – the first use of a substitute in an FA Cup Final. At ninety minutes it was 0-0 and the game went into extra time.

West Brom's Jeff Astle had scored in every round of the cup campaign. In the 93rd minute, he continued his success by scoring the only goal of the match.

Liverpool FC

Reds legend Billy Liddell leads out the stars for his testimonial match at Anfield in September 1960. Behind Billy are Tom Finney and Bert Trautman. In a career spanning sixteen years, Liddell made 537 appearances for Liverpool, scoring 229 goals.

(Bottom). It is estimated that around 20,000 viewers tuned into BBC2 *Match of the Day* on 22 August 1964 to watch highlights of the Division One game between Liverpool and Arsenal from Anfield. No one on Merseyside could watch the game as BBC2 625-line TV was not transmitted outside the London area. In any case the BBC considered it nothing more than a trial transmission for intended coverage of the 1966 World Cup. Yet from these humble beginnings at Anfield emerged the world's longest-running TV programme dedicated to football. The decision was taken to move *Match of the Day* to BBC1, though a number of clubs were not happy as they believed prior publicity would impact upon gates. The agreement reached between the Football League and the BBC was that the game to be shown on Saturday night TV would not be announced until all that afternoon's fixtures had been completed. Our image shows Gerry Byrne hotly pursued by Terry Anderson. Full-back Ronnie Moran opened the scoring for Liverpool in the eleventh minute.

Liverpool v Arsenal, 22 August 1964. Just four minutes into the second half, Gordon Wallace – who made only twenty first team appearances for Liverpool between 1962-67 - leaped high to head the ball over keeper Jim Furnell and into the net for the Reds' second goal. Three minutes from time, he scored again to make it 3-2.

(Middle). Liverpool v Arsenal, 22 August 1964. Panic amid the Gunners' defence. Keeper Jim Furnell, somewhat harassed by Roger Hunt, looks on as Don Howe manages the clear the ball from the goal line.

(Bottom left). Liverpool v Arsenal, 22 August 1964. The very first *Match of the Day* was interrupted by a pitch invasion. Not by fans but a cat that briefly occupied the Liverpool goalmouth.

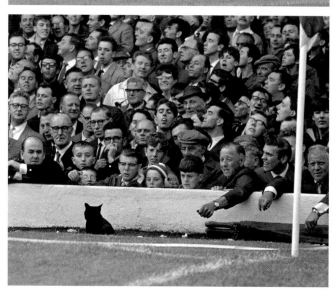

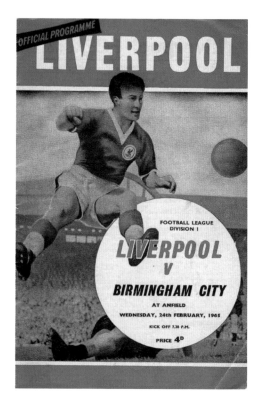

On 27 March 1965, Liverpool faced Chelsea at Villa Park in one of the 1965 FA Cup semi-finals. It is said that before kick-off Bill Shankly happened to come across a copy of the design for a brochure Chelsea were going to produce should they reach the final. He pinned it up in the Reds' dressing room and told his players to "Stuff those wee cocky south buggers." Which they did 2-0. Here Reds fans go a bit wild following the final whistle.

(Bottom). Liverpool pose for a team photograph at Anfield. Back row, left to right: Gordon Milne, Gerry Byrne, Tommy Lawrence, Ron Yeats, Chris Lawler and Willie Stevenson. Front row, left to right: Ian Callaghan, Roger Hunt, Ian St John, Tommy Smith and Peter Thompson.

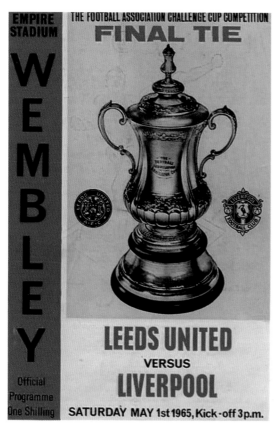

The 1965 FA Cup Final against Leeds United. Within a few minutes of the kick-off, full-back Gerry Byrne broke his collar-bone but carried on as these were the days before substitutes – a brave decision given the opposition's reputation for hard tackling. With neither side giving much away, though Gary Sprake was forced to make a couple of saves, there was no score after 90 minutes and for the first time since 1947 the FA Cup Final went into extra time.

Three minutes into extra-time and the game suddenly changed as Gerry Byrne fired a cross from the right-hand side of the pitch for Roger Hunt to head home. Seven minutes later, Billy Bremner fired home the equaliser. There were nine minutes remaining when Ian Callaghan brought the fans to life with a centre that Ian St John met to head in the winner.

(Middle). 1965 FA Cup Final. Tommy Smith slides in to tackle Norman Hunter.

(Bottom). 1965 FA Cup Final. Tommy Smith and Ian Callaghan block out Albert Johanneson.

Bill Shankly and the team return following their victory over Leeds United. Winning the FA Cup qualified Liverpool to take part in the 1965-66 European Cup-winners' Cup. Before then, however, and only three days after appearing at Wembley, Liverpool faced Inter Milan in the first leg of the European Cup semi-final. After only four minutes, the Reds went ahead when Roger Hunt converted a cross from Ian Callaghan. Before half-time, Milan had equalised, only for Ian Callaghan to put Liverpool 2-1 up thanks to a pass from Roger Hunt. The Reds should have gone 3-1 up but Chris Lawler had what looked like a perfect gaol disallowed for offside. During the second half, the game flowed from end to end but in the 75th minute Ian St John got a foot to a rebound and put the ball in the net. Liverpool travelled to Milan 3-1 up for the second-leg, where, in front of 90,000 fans, they lost 3-0. Milan went through to the final 4-3 on aggregate.

Though Inter Milan ended Liverpool's run in the 1964-65 European Cup, the Reds had not only qualified for the 1965-66 European Cup-winners' Cup but had gone on to reach the final by beating Juventus, Standard Liege, Honved and Celtic. On 5 May 1966, at Hampden Park, they faced German side Borussia Dortmund. Despite having a capacity of 100,000, only 41,657 fans turned up to watch. The game was 0-0 at half time but in the 61st minute, Sigfried Held put Dortmund in the lead. Seven minutes later Roger Hunt equalised. The score remained 1-1 at the end of 90 minutes and the game went into extra time. In the 107th minute of play, Tommy Lawrence cleared the ball only for it to find Reinhard Libuda who fired a shot at goal from 35yards. The ball went over Lawrence and Ron Yeats, rebounded off the post, hit Yeats and bounced into the goal. Liverpool's run in Europe was over for the time being. They would however be back.

(Above). Liverpool v Borussia Dortmund, 5 May 1966. The ball skims over Dortmund's goal after being headed by their defender Theodor Redder.

(Above right). The 1966 FA Charity Shield was an all Merseyside affair between Liverpool and Everton at Goodison Park. Before the game – which Liverpool won 1-0 - the World Cup, FA Cup and Football League Trophy were paraded around the ground. This image shows members of the World Cup-winning England squad, Gerry Byrne, Ian Callaghan, Roger Hunt and Everton's Ray Wilson, showing off the silver tankards presented to them by the Lord Mayor of Liverpool.

(Opposite page top). 31 December 1966 and 53,744 fans have turned up to Anfield to watch Liverpool play Everton in a game that ended 0-0. Everton's Alan Ball is chased by Ron Yeats and Tommy Smith. It had been an interesting month for Liverpool. A 1-0 home win against Sheffield Wednesday on 3 December was followed up a week later with a 2-2 draw at Old Trafford. On Christmas Eve, Liverpool were away to Chelsea where they won 2-1 and on Boxing Day Chelsea were at Anfield, where again they lost 2-1.

(Opposite page bottom). Craven Cottage on 25 February 1967, and Bobby Robson and Ian St John are in a race for the ball. Liverpool's away form so far that season had been better than most, having taken 16 points from 15 games. Since the beginning of the year, their away form had seen them win 1-0 at Sheffield Wednesday, lose 2-1 at Leicester City and draw 2-2 at Sunderland. This game ended 2-2.

(Left). A youthful Ray Clemence pictured at Anfield shortly after being signed for £15,000 from Scunthorpe United. His first senior appearance was at Anfield on 25 September 1968 when the Reds played Swansea Town in the Third Round of the League Cup. Tommy Lawrence remained first choice between the posts for the 1968-69 season and it was not until 31 January 1970 that Clemence made his League debut in an away fixture against Nottingham Forest. He made his League debut at home on 28 February in the 0-2 defeat by Derby County.

(Bottom left). Only 31,713 fans were at Anfield on 9 September 1959 to see Roger Hunt score on his League debut in a Second Division game against Scunthorpe United. During the 1961-62 season, he scored 41 goals in 41 games, helping the club to the Second Division title, eight points clear of runners up Leyton Orient. His prowess in front of goal made him the club's top scorer for eight seasons. By the end of the decade he held two club records: leading scoring record for a single season (41 goals), and the League aggregate of 245 goals in 401 full appearances. By the time he left for Bolton Wanderers in 1969, he had amassed 285 goals out of a total of 484 appearances plus five as a substitute for Liverpool – a record that would stand for more than two decades.

(Bottom right). Ian Callaghan, who had cost Liverpool the princely sum of a £10 signing-on fee, made his first senior appearance in the same season as Roger Hunt, when he replaced Billy Liddell for the Second Division game against Bristol Rovers on 16 April 1960. However, it was not until the 1961-62 season that he became a regular first team choice. His first game that season was the away tie against Preston North End on 4 November, during which he scored his first goal in a senior game. He made a further 23 League appearances that season and remained an automatic choice for the remainder of the decade.

By the time Liverpool journeyed to the Baseball Ground to face First Division newcomers Derby County on 1 November 1969, they had played seventeen League games, won nine, drawn six, and lost only two – 1-0 at Old Trafford and 1-0 at Newcastle United. In their previous fixture on 25 October, the Reds had beaten Southampton at Anfield. It had been 1-1 with just seven minutes remaining when Roger Hunt put Liverpool ahead in the 83rd minute. The Reds were still celebrating when he scored again in the 84th minute. An own goal by Byrne in the 88th minute made it 4-1.

On paper, 1968-69 First Division runners-up Liverpool possibly had the edge but they were facing Derby County on their home turf; a side inspired by their charismatic manager Brian Clough. Also, they were playing at the Baseball Ground, a compact and sometimes notoriously muddy venue, sandwiched between a foundry and rows of terraced houses. Just under 41,000 fans were there to witness the Rams inflict what would be Liverpool's biggest defeat of the season. Our image shows Ron Yeats blocking a shot from Derby forward Kevin Hector.

(Left). Despite Derby winning 4-0, the game was not one-sided. Here Derby's keeper Les Green, supported by right-back Ron Webster and centre-half Roy MacFarland, close down a Liverpool attack.

(Bottom). The look on Bobby Moore's face says it all as full back Chris Lawler opens the scoring in the 27th minute for Liverpool in their match against West Ham at Anfield on 15 November 1969. Bobby Graham made it 2-0 in the 60th minute to give the Reds both points. Chris Lawler was one of the decade's outstanding full-backs, willing to take advantage of the play to move up front and have a crack at goal. He signed as a junior in 1960, making his League debut during the 1962-63 season. In 546 appearances for Liverpool he scored 61 goals, eleven of them in European games. During the 1969-70 season, his was the only name on the score sheet in four games where Liverpool took both points. On 30 August 1969, he scored the only goal in the game against Sheffield Wednesday. On 17 January 1970, he scored the only goal in the match against West Bromwich Albion. It was the same again on 30 March against Wolves and on 15 April against Sunderland.

Tranmere Rovers FC

It's trebles all round as Tranmere Rovers celebrate their 3-1 win over Rochdale on 12 May 1967 and with it almost certain promotion to the Third Division. It was not for want of trying. The 1964-65 season ended with Tranmere in 5th place, just one point adrift of Oxford United. The 1965-66 season was possibly even more frustrating. Again, they finished in 5th place, tying with Colchester United on 56 points but losing out on goal difference. Under the guidance of manager David Russell, Tranmere approached the 1966-67 with the same gritty determination that had seen them come so close to promotion over the previous two seasons.

Two players were given a chance to establish themselves in the first team - Central defender Roy McFarland and George Hudson, a centre forward with plenty of experience having played for Blackburn Rovers, Accrington Stanley, Coventry City and Northampton Town.

Russell also proved astute at obtaining the services of centre forward George Yardley on a free transfer from Luton Town. During four years with Tranmere, Yardley would make 123 senior domestic appearances, scoring 68 goals. The other player Russell signed was left-winger Graham Williams who had made 31 senior domestic appearances for Everton during 1956-59 but had recently been with non-League Wellington Town. He would go on to make 74 senior domestic appearances before moving to Port Vale in 1968.

The 1966-67 season opened on 20 August with a home fixture against Chester City which ended 0-0. The next game, an away tie at Bradford City, finished with Tranmere losing 1-0. It was a wake-up call. After that, Tranmere went thirteen League games without defeat, including beating Crewe Alexandra 5-0. After a mid-season wobble, including losing 1-2 at home to Barrow on 17 March and by the same margin a week later at home to Southend United, Tranmere got their act together, losing just one of their last twelve games – 1-2 at home to Southport on 28 April.

(Opposite page continued). The season ended with Tranmere having won 22, drawn 14 and lost 10. They were in 4th place on 58 points. Stockport County had taken the Fourth Division title with 64points, Southport and Barrow tied on 59 points though Southport had the better goal difference.

On 9 December 1967, they faced Rochdale in the First Round Proper of the FA Cup. This was the round where the Third and Fourth Division sides joined the non-league clubs that had survived the qualifying rounds. Tranmere went through 5-1, drawing an away fixture against Fourth Division strugglers Bradford Park Avenue in the next round. Played on 6 January 1968, the game ended in a 2-3 victory for the Merseysiders, putting then in the Third Round for the first time since 1963.

The Third Round was when the First and Second divisions joined the competition. Tranmere drew Second Division Huddersfield Town at home and 20,038 fans turned up to Prenton Park to watch the home side go through 2-1. The win put Tranmere into the Fourth Round for the first time since 1952, when they had been drawn away to First Division Chelsea at Stamford Bridge. In 1952, Chelsea had brought Tranmere's dreams of cup glory to an abrupt end with a 4-0 hammering, so drawing First Division Coventry City away must have been met with mixed emotions. Played on 17 February, the game ended 1-1. Coventry manager Noel Cantwell put his side's failure to win down to being without centre-half Maurice Setters and cup-tied striker Neil Martin. He also thought Tranmere's 87th minute equaliser should have been disallowed.

When the teams faced one another just four days later in the replay at Prenton Park, they knew that the winner would face Everton at Goodison Park on 9 March.

(This page). There were about fifteen minutes of the first-half remaining when Coventry City centre-half Maurice Setters gathered the ball in Coventry's penalty area. He had plenty of time to clear it but miskicked it. The ball bounced off George Yardley and into the path of George Hudson, who hammered it in with his left foot from 20yards.

Only five minutes after George Hudson's goal, George Yardley received a pass from Denis Stevens and slipped deftly past Coventry's John Tudor to put the ball into the net to make it 2-0. Desperation gripped Noel Cantwell's men. Coventry went in for offside traps and a bit of heavy tackling that saw Setters booked for flattening George Yardley and Tranmere's Stan Storton booked for retaliation. Tranmere kept up the pressure and could have had two more goals at the very least.

One young fan got so carried away that he leaped on the back of George Hudson, seen in our image congratulating George Yardley.

For the first time in the club's history, Tranmere Rovers had reached the Fifth Round of the FA Cup. They were in good company. Of the sixteen surviving clubs, eleven were from the First Division: Sheffield Wednesday, Chelsea, Everton, Liverpool, Spurs, West Brom, Arsenal, Sheffield Utd, West Ham, Leicester City and Leeds United. There were four Second Division clubs still in the fight: Rotherham United, Portsmouth, Birmingham City and Bristol City. Tranmere Rovers were the sole survivors from the Third and Fourth Divisions.

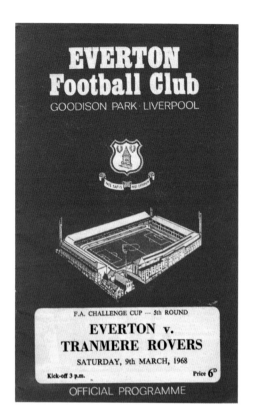

(Top right). In front of 61,982 fans, Johnny Morrisey recovers the ball from the back of the net after teammate Joe Royle had opened the scoring in the FA Cup Fifth Round tie. Johnny Morrisey scored Everton's second goal. The game ended 2-0.

(Middle). Tranmere keeper Jim Cumbes goes up high to grab the ball away from John Hurst and Joe Royle.

(Bottom right). Jim Cumbes to the rescue again has he pulls off a flying save.

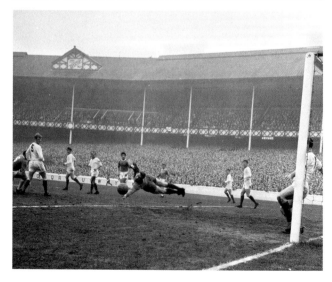

During the 1964 Grand National, jockey Paddy Farrell was thrown from his horse *Border Flight* at the fifteenth fence. Farrell broke his back and was confined to a wheelchair.

Tim Norman and the 50/1 outsider *Anglo* clear the last, going on to win the 1966 Grand National by twenty lengths. *Anglo's* time for the race was 9minutes 52.8seconds, which would turn out to be the slowest for the decade – though not by much as the 1962 winner *Kilmore* (ridden by Fred Winter) took 9 minutes 50seconds, and the 1967 winner Foinavon (ridden by John Buckingham) took 9 minutes 49.6seconds. Our second image features *Anglo* and fourth placed *The Fossa* (ridden by Tim Biddlecombe) after the race.

Safely over the first for the 1967 Grand National is No.8 *Kilburn*, ridden by Tim Norman from, at far right, No.6 *Solbina*, ridden by Eddie Harty. Partially hidden is No.13 *Greek Scholar*, ridden by Terry Biddlecombe and the grey is No.12 *Forecastle*, ridden by Nimrod Wilkinson. *Greek Scholar* came in in fourth place at 20/1, two places ahead of 25/1 *Solbina*. The 50/1 outsider *Forecastle* was pulled up at the sixteenth and heavily backed *Kilburn* fell at the nineteenth.

(Top). The possibility of *Foinavon* winning the 1967 Grand National was akin to Tranmere Rovers winning the European Cup. So unfancied in fact that *Foinavon* was brought to Aintree on race day. Of the forty-four starters, twenty-eight had made it safely over the 22nd fence, including a loose horse *Popham Down*. At the 23rd, *Popham Down* suddenly veered right, hampering *Rutherfords* and unseating its jockey Johnny Leech. Chaos followed as horses fell or refused and riders were unseated. Meanwhile, 100/1 outsider *Foinavon*, which had made a slow start and was lagging behind the leaders, approached the pile-up but jockey John Buckingham was able to find a small gap for a clean jump. *Foinavon* was suddenly thirty lengths ahead, though Josh Gifford managed to remount the 15/2 favourite *Honey End* and give chase. Foinavon won by fifteen lengths, *Honey End* was second, *Red Alligator* third, and *Greek Scholar* fourth. The Tote paid 444/1 on the result.

It was the first time in twenty years that a 100/1 outsider had won the National. The previous occasion, when *Caughoo* won by twenty lengths in 1947, was surrounded in controversy. The race had taken place in thick fog and *Caughoo's* jockey Eddie Dempsey was accused of cheating. It was claimed that he had taken advantage of the fog to hide behind one of the fences, coming out toward the end. It was only some years later that photographs appeared proving *Caughoo* had indeed run the race and Dempsey's name was cleared.

(Middle). *Foinavon* is surrounded in the winner's enclosure after the race.

(Bottom). It was glorious sunshine and perfect going for the 45 runners taking part in the 1968 Grand National. Roy Edwards and *The Fossa* – seen here clearing the water jump from *Rondetto, San Angello, Princeful* and *Rutherfords* - led most of the way but began to fade after jumping Valentines for the second time. Brian Fletcher on *Red Alligator* went ahead, building a lead of twenty lengths from Barry Brogan on *Moidore's Token*, David Mould on *Different Class* and Pat Buckley on *Rutherfords*. *The Fossa* finished fifth.

Amateur rider Tim Durrant and *Highlandie*. At 68, Tim was the oldest rider in the race. They came in in fifteenth place.

Brian Fletcher and *Red Alligator* win the 1968 Grand National by twenty lengths.

It is into Beechers for the second time in the 1969 National and *Steel Bridge* (33) jumps ahead of *Highland Wedding* (14), and *The Fossa* (20). It was all over for *Kilburn* (7) and jockey Tommy Carberry and *Tam Kiss* was brought down a few seconds later. *Rondetto* is the horse jumping Beechers.

(Top). The Fourteenth RAC British Grand Prix (1961), run in conjunction with the *Daily Mirror,* started in appalling conditions – it was hard to believe it was the 15 July. The skies were solid grey and the heavens had opened just fifteen minutes before the start of the 225mile race over 75 laps. Spray mixed with heavy rain made driving difficult for the tail-enders. The race was just five laps old when Henry Taylor, driving a Lotus-Climax for the UDT Laystall Racing Team, came sideways out of Melling Crossing, spun and crashed into a hoarding. This was Taylor's eleventh, and final, Formula One Championship race. He was badly injured by a wooden stake from the hoarding that had gone through the side of his car. Taylor took up rallying, taking part in the Monte Carlo Rally. He also drove for the Ford Works Team and was at the wheel when the Ford Cortina made its rally debut.

(Right). Wolfgang Alexander Albert Eduard Maximilian Reichsgraf Berghe von Trips (better known to motor racing fans as Taffy von Trips and the winner of the 1961 British Grand Prix) shakes hands with *Daily Mirror* editor Lee Howard. Von Trips had led for much of the 75-lap race after starting from fourth position on the grid. Von Trips and Ferrari teammates Phil Hill and Richie Ginther took first, second and third. Jack Brabham was fourth.

On 10 September, the Italian Grand Prix was held at Monza and third place would have been enough to give von Trips the 1961 World Championship. However, on the first lap he collided with Jim Clark's Lotus. The Ferrari careered across the grass verge and up an embankment, hitting the fence on the top. The rear of the Ferrari lifted and the car then spun round a couple of times, scything down spectators before plunging upside down onto the verge with such force that it bounced into the air and landed right way up across the track. Fourteen spectators as well as von Trips were killed.

(Top). For the 1961 season, the Rob Walker Racing Team entered their Ferguson P99 – Climax, unique in that it was the first four-wheel drive and the last front-engined car to be entered in a Formula One Championship race. The race started with Jack Fairman at the wheel and though the car's four-wheel drive helped road holding in the appalling conditions, Fairman began experiencing ignition problems in the fifth lap shortly after passing the wreckage of Henry Taylor's Lotus-Climax. Fairman was convinced there was a short circuit somewhere but the pit staff changed the plugs and off he went again. He was soon back in the pits and proved right. A wire was shorting against the chassis, probably caused when running over debris from Taylor's Lotus.

During lap 44, the team's Lotus-Climax which was being driven by Stirling Moss had to be retired due to problems with its brakes – they were almost non-existent. Twelve laps later, Fairman was back in the pits with technical problems. Unfortunately, the mechanics gave him a push start and the stewards had no choice but to disqualify the car for trackside assistance. The team had a word with the stewards and the Ferguson was allowed to continue for evaluation purposes only, Stirling Moss taking over as it was considered he would push the car to its limits.

(Middle). Taffy von Trips, driving a Ferrari, leads Stirling Moss out of Tatts Corner. Von Trips went on to win and Ferrari would take first, second and third places.

(Bottom).1962 British Grand Prix. Jim Clark in his Lotus 25-Climax laps the Porsche 718 of Jonkheer Karel Pieter Antoni Jan Hubertus Godin de Beaufort – otherwise known as Carel Godin de Beaufort. The Dutch nobleman was a true amateur, his Ecurie Maarsbergen Racing Team taking its name from his family estate. Somewhat eccentric, he often drove barefoot and undertook his practice laps for the 1964 German Grand Prix wearing a Beatles wig instead of a helmet. It was at the 1964 German Grand Prix that he sustained fatal injuries when his car left the track at the notorious Berwerk Corner. Thrown clear, he suffered severe injuries to his head and chest, dying the following evening in hospital in Cologne.

Jack Brabham had hoped to race his own car – the Brabham-Climax V8 - and though his mechanics had worked on it until the wee small hours of the morning of the race, it lacked the correct exhaust so he decided to drive his Lotus-Climax. Brabham managed fifth place despite being in considerable pain for 32 laps after suffering burns to his right foot.

Jim Clark on the grid in pole position for the 1962 British Grand Prix after setting a new Aintree lap record of 1min 53.6secs during qualifying. He led from start to finish recording the fastest lap – 1min 55secs (93.913mph).

A pair of Ferrari 156 Formula One racing cars attract a small crowd prior to the start of the *Daily Mirror* sponsored Aintree 200 on Saturday 27 April 1963. It would be the first time that season that World Champion Graham Hill and runner-up Jim Clark would be going head-to-head. Clark's latest Lotus was fitted with a new Climax fuel injected V8 engine developing 200bhp, making it much faster than his 1962 car. Clark had already hit 95.74mph during practice – faster than the official lap record he had set during the previous year's 200. Clark's assessment was that his Lotus and Hill's BRM were evenly matched.

THE RUGBY LEAGUE CHALLENGE CUP COMPETITION

FINAL TIE

HULL KINGSTON ROVERS
v
WIDNES

SATURDAY MAY, 9th 1964   Kick-off 3 p.m.

WEMBLEY

EMPIRE STADIUM

OFFICIAL PROGRAMME · · · ONE SHILLING

(Top left). Widnes take on Hull Kingston Rovers in the RL Challenge Cup Final at Wembley on 9 May 1964. Getting to the final had been something of a marathon for the Chemics. The First Round went to two replays before they could dispose of Leigh. In the Second Round, they beat Liverpool City at the first attempt, but the Third Round against Swinton also went to a replay. Even the semi-final against Castleford went to a replay, which Widnes won 15-3. Here, Widnes skipper Vince Karalius moves in to block a Hull KR attack.

(Middle). Jim Measures tangles with the Hull KR defence giving Frank Collier time and room to sprint away and score Widnes's last try of the game. The final score was Widnes 13, Hull KR 5. It was the third time in their history that Widnes had won the Challenge Cup, having beaten St Helens 10-3 in 1930 and Keighley 18-5 in 1937. The club appeared in the 1950 final against Warrington but were thrashed 19-0. The 1964 Challenge Cup was their first trophy for eighteen years. It was also their only major success of the decade. Jim Measures played 133 games for Widnes, scoring 47 tries. In 1963, he was capped twice for Great Britain against Australia.

(Bottom). Holding the cup aloft are Vince Karalius (left) and Lance Todd trophy winner Frank Collier. Born in Widnes, loose-forward Vince Karalius joined Widnes in 1962, playing 128 games and scoring six tries. Frank Collier joined Widnes in 1964 and played 64 games for them, scoring five tries.

(Opposite page top). This image slightly predates the 1960s, but it features one of Liverpool's greatest boxers, Hogan 'Kid' Bassey, who retired from the ring in 1959. Born in Nigeria, Okon Bassey Asuquo already held the West African and Nigerian Bantamweight titles when he moved to Liverpool, the city he would spend most of his life in. Adopting the name Hogan Bassey, he had 74 professional fights. His first in the UK was against Ray Hillyard in Liverpool on 31 January 1952. On 19 November 1955, he knocked out Billy 'Spider' Kelly to take the Commonwealth Featherweight title and a technical knockout against Cherif Hamia in Paris on 24 June 1957 gave him the World Featherweight title. Hogan had seventeen bouts in Liverpool, winning fifteen. On 18 March 1959, he lost his World Featherweight title to Davey Moore. He also lost the rematch a few months later on 19 August. Our image shows him with his wife and Liverpool MP Bessie Braddock outside Buckingham Palace after receiving his MBE from the Queen.

(Opposite page bottom). Heavyweights Jim Monaghan (Derry) and Lloyd Walford (Jamaica) battle it out at The Stadium Arena on 20 September 1965. This was their second fight in six months, having fought at Ulster Hall, Belfast, on 30 March, when Monaghan won on points. Roles were reversed at the Stadium – Walford won on points.

Jim Monaghan had a relatively short professional career – just nineteen bouts fought between 1963-66. His professional debut was in his home town, where he fought John Spenceley at the Guild Hall, on 22 October 1963. It ended in a draw. The Walford bout was Monaghan's second visit to The Stadium, having fought Carl Gizzi there on 1 February 1965. Monaghan lost on points. The Irishman's last fight was against Barney Wilson for the vacant BBBofC Northern Ireland Area Heavyweight Title at the Ulster Hall, Belfast, on 22 November 1966. Monaghan lost by a technical knockout.

Lloyd Walford made his professional debut in a bout against Roy Seward at Sincil Bank (Lincoln City FC's ground), Lincoln, on 6 July 1964. He lost by a technical knockout. As well as his fight against Monaghan, Walford had two more bouts at The Stadium. On 27 October 1966, he knocked out Doug Fowler and on 11 April 1968 he lost on points to Ray Ako. Walford's last fight, against John L Gardner, was at the Royal Albert Hall, Kensington, on 20 January 1976. Walford was knocked out.

Emile Griffith of the USA takes a break during a training session in preparation for his fight against Liverpool's Harry Scott at the Royal Albert Hall, Kensington. Both were seasoned campaigners. Griffith was World Welterweight Champion and a veteran of 54 fights of which he had won 46 and lost seven with one no-contest.

Harry Scott had had 47 fights, had won 27, lost sixteen, and drawn four. He was the holder of the BBBofC Central Area Middleweight Title, having beaten Sid Parkinson for the vacant title, and defended against challengers Jim Swords and Alf Mathews. The Griffith v Scott bout on 4 October ended in the seventh when the Liverpudlian retired. Scott's professional career began at The Stadium, Liverpool, where on 2 June 1960 he defeated Jimmy Asani by a technical knockout. Before the year was out, Scott had had two more bouts at The Stadium, beating both Neil McAteer and Malcolm Worthington. Scott's fights in Liverpool during 1961 included return bouts against Malcolm Worthington and Neil McAteer. He also knocked out Yolandie Pompey and drew against Charlie Cotton.

Scott was on his home turf for his first bout of 1962 when he knocked out relative newcomer Henry Speedie at The Stadium on 30 January. Fans then had to wait until December to see Scott fight in Liverpool again, when he secured a win on points against Felipe Aleyeto. Scott's next bout in Liverpool was a successful defence of his middleweight title against Alf Mathews on 28 January 1965. Though Harry Scott would continue to box professionally until his defeat by Trevor Francis on 13 June 1973, he fought only three more times in Liverpool - against Ruben Orrico on 11 July 1967, Les McAteer on 17 September 1968 and William Poitrimol on 18 May 1971.

(Top left). Arnold Palmer sizing up a putt during the 1965 British Open at Royal Birkdale Golf Club, Southport.

(Above). Tomy Lema driving off at the 1st, 16th Ryder Cup, 1965.

(Above right). Australian Peter Thompson walks through having missed a long putt for a three at the Par five, 513yard 18th during the first round on 7 July. Thompson had won the 1954, 1955, 1956 and 1958 Opens and 1965 would be the year he won his fifth claret jug, finishing at -7 to Par and two strokes ahead of runners-up Brian Huggett and Christy O'Connor Snr. The total prize money was £10,000 with £1750 going to the winner. Huggett and O'Connor each got £1125.